THE
**ROBERT GORDON
UNIVERSITY**
ABERDEEN

HISTORIC SCOTLAND

STONE CLEANING

A GUIDE FOR PRACTITIONERS

CHRISTOPHER ANDREW

AND

MAUREEN YOUNG
KENNETH TONGE
THE MASONRY CONSERVATION RESEARCH GROUP. THE ROBERT GORDON UNIVERSITY
(DIRECTOR DENNIS URQUHART)

IN ASSOCIATION WITH

TECHNICAL CONSERVATION, RESEARCH AND EDUCATION DIVISION. HISTORIC SCOTLAND
(DIRECTOR INGVAL MAXWELL)

Masonry Conservation Research Group

A multidisciplinary research group undertaking research in the field of masonry conservation.
The original team members who contributed to the research for this volume were:-

Christopher Andrew
Seaton Baxter
John MacDonald
Bruce Thomson
Kenneth Tonge
Dennis Urquhart
Robin Webster
Maureen Young

In addition group membership consists of:-

Melanie Jones
Richard Laing
Keith Nicholson
Rachael Wakefield

Historic Scotland

David Brown
Peter Donaldson
Ingval Maxwell

Scottish Enterprise

John Gould
John Lindsay

The author is grateful to the following individuals and organisations for assistance and comments made on earlier drafts of the manuscript.

Craig Liddle, Stone Federation, Great Britain.
Desmond Hodges, Director, Edinburgh New Town Conservation Committee.
Bill McConnell, R.I.C.S. Building Surveyor's Division.
Planning Department, Glasgow City Council.

Note

Publication Details

Cover Picture: Randolph Crescent, Edinburgh.

First Edition 1994. ISBN   0 7480 0874 8

© Historic Scotland & The Robert Gordon University.

Contents

Introduction

Stonecleaning: an overview

Of all the changes to which buildings can be subjected, stonecleaning is one of the most visually dramatic. It is a process which changes not only the fundamental appearance of buildings but also the environmental context in which these buildings exist.

Over the last decade, stonecleaning has grown into a multimillion pound industry, although the history of stonecleaning can be traced back much further. Much of the more recent stonecleaning activity has taken place as part of urban renewal and regeneration programmes. Without the visual improvements which stonecleaning has brought about, valuable parts of the urban fabric may well have been lost to redevelopment. Stonecleaning work has been encouraged by a number of grant awarding bodies, partly because of the assumed aesthetic benefits which are thought to accrue from stonecleaning, and also as an attempt to regenerate economically depressed urban areas. Stonecleaning has brought about dramatic improvements in the appearance of many urban buildings, particularly in cities blackened by the industrial pollution of the past. The colour of stonework and the architectural detailing of buildings becomes more apparent following cleaning. The net result of this activity has been to stimulate a pride and interest in our architectural heritage which it is difficult to imagine any other activity doing to the same extent. Stonecleaning has also had a less tangible "psychological" effect in urban areas. For example, following stonecleaning the reflected light at street level is increased, leading to a brighter, less oppressive atmosphere. The inhabitants of many tenement properties have welcomed the improvement to their living conditions which stonecleaning has brought. In many cases these improvements have been part of general refurbishment programmes.

Whilst the visual improvements brought about by stonecleaning should not be underestimated, neither should be the dangers. Increasingly, concerns have been expressed at the irreversible damage caused to some buildings by stonecleaning. Evidence abounds of situations where unskilled operatives, using inappropriate techniques and undue haste have caused permanent damage to buildings. The situation is often exacerbated by the process of tendering for stonecleaning contracts, where the unwary client simply choses the lowest tender price without detailed consideration of the possible implications of that decision. In this situation the reputable stonecleaning company, which is more likely to devote greater time, care and resources to the contract, cannot match the price of the unscrupulous operator whose motivation is solely financial. The consequence of this has been that some of the more reputable companies have withdrawn from stonecleaning work, leaving the way clear for the less scrupulous.

Whilst in the past there have been no established mechanisms in place for the training or licensing of stonecleaning contractors, this is currently being addressed by the more reputable companies and the standard setting bodies. However, it is possible to purchase, without restriction, equipment and chemicals capable of doing great damage to masonry.

Research basis for the guide

Concern at the damage done by stonecleaning has centred around a number of issues. These have mainly involved the lack of scientific knowledge and the possible long term effects. It is widely accepted that where buildings are cleaned, the process should be carried out by competent practitioners with the appropriate knowledge base and skills, particularly where buildings important to the national heritage are involved. The evidence so far suggests that sections of the industry have some way to go in reaching acceptable standards. In 1989, partly as a response to this growing unease, Historic Scotland and Scottish Enterprise commissioned the Masonry Conservation Research Group at The Robert Gordon University to undertake research into the physical, chemical and aesthetic effects of the cleaning of sandstone buildings. In 1992 the results of this research were published (Webster *et al.*,1992).

The guide for practitioners

Following publication of the research findings, the Masonry Conservation Research Group undertook a further commission to produce this guide, based on the research report and the proceedings of the stonecleaning international conference (Webster, 1992) . The aim in writing this guide has been to help those involved in stonecleaning to make better informed decisions, thus avoiding some of the mistakes and damage which has occurred in the past. The guide follows from the Historic Scotland publication; Memorandum of Guidance on Listed Buildings and Conservation Areas (1993), giving further clarification on issues relating to stonecleaning.

Every building considered for stonecleaning will differ over a range of parameters including, for example, stone type, surface texture, architectural style, microclimates, and the nature and pattern of soiling. As such, each will pose a different set of problems when cleaning is being considered. As a result, it has not always been possible to give answers to specific questions but, by considering these guidelines, the practitioner should arrive at a more appropriate solution to many of the problems likely to be encountered.

It should be stressed that many of the problems highlighted in this guide should not occur if, following an informed decision to proceed with cleaning, the work is carried out by skilled, properly trained personnel, using appropriate methods and following set guidelines. However, the end result of stonecleaning is very much dependent on the skill of individual operatives working with a comprehensive knowledge of the processes involved. The approach adopted throughout this guide is one which stresses that any stonecleaning undertaken should result in as little damage as possible to the fabric of buildings.

If the damage caused and mistakes made in the past are to be avoided, the standards within some sections of the stonecleaning industry must be raised. This will mean commitment within the industry to a number of changes. A key element will be the continual updating of the knowledge base as a result of on-going research into stonecleaning, as well as changes in working practice as a result of improving knowledge. The training needs of those actively involved in stonecleaning must be accurately identified and met. Additionally, the care and attention given to stonecleaning work must, at the very least, be on a par with the range of other work undertaken by the building industry. Where stonecleaning forms part of a contract of work, the proportion of the budget devoted to this activity should reflect its importance.

If standards are to be improved, there must also be commitment from building professionals, planning authorities and clients. All professionals must be more aware of the aesthetic and physical implications of the stonecleaning work with which they are involved. The formulation of appropriate specifications, based on reliable and relevant scientific data, as well as close supervision of work are paramount. Planning authorities should set up data bases in which to hold information from the inspection of stonework and reports produced in connection with the application to clean and any subsequent cleaning activity. This will enable authorities gradually to build up a store of knowledge which will help them to assess the risks and predict areas of potential damage when an application is submitted. Clients must also be prepared to fund stonecleaning work at a level which reflects the need for improved standards. Some of the damage caused by stonecleaning in the past is the responsibility of clients, who have demanded unrealistic, and often undesirable levels of cleanliness from stonecleaning.

Stonecleaning is a complex issue. In the past some stonecleaning work has been undertaken without sufficient thought to the consequences. The issues involved and the historic value of much of the architecture which is stonecleaned, demands careful consideration from all parties. This guide for practitioners will help those involved in stonecleaning make more fully informed decisions.

Chapter 1   Sandstones

1.1 Sandstone

Sandstone is a sedimentary rock. It is formed from mineral grains derived from the erosion of pre-existing rocks, which are transported, then deposited in a sedimentary basin by the action of water, wind or ice. The grains are either held together with a cement or embedded in a fine grained silty matrix (Figure 1.1). The types of mineral grains in a sandstone are highly variable. The most common constituent is quartz. It is the principle constituent of most sandstones and may, in some rare cases, constitute 100% of the rock. Other mineral types commonly found in sandstone include feldspars, micas, clay minerals, carbonates and iron oxides. Rock fragments are also relatively common. Sediments can also include organic material, chemical precipitates (salts) and volcanic ashes. Although the list of commonly occurring minerals in sandstones is relatively short, in principle almost any known mineral may occur. The minerals most commonly found in sandstones are those which are most resistant to decay and are best able to survive the processes of erosion, transportation and deposition.

The formation of sandstones

Sedimentary rocks are formed in layers which accumulate on top of each other over long periods of time. Sedimentary units are seldom flat and uniform. There are a wide variety of sedimentary structures which can cause local variations in the characteristics of a sandstone. The most common of these are ripples and dunes, formed when sands are deposited by water or wind currents. These structures are seen in sandstones as cross-bedding. Deformational structures can also form after deposition due to movements within the sediment.

The size of particles which make up sandstone vary between about 0.06 and 2 mm in diameter. The grains within an individual sandstone may be uniform in their size distribution. More often, a mixture of differently sized particles occurs. As sand grains are transported they become more rounded. Sandstones formed of grains derived from a local source tend to contain a mixture of angular grains. If the grains are transported for longer distances or for a greater length of time before deposition, they become more rounded, and less resistant minerals are lost, leaving the sediment dominated by quartz. After deposition the sediment consists of loose sand grains and pore spaces filled with air or water. As the sediment becomes buried, processes of lithification turn the sediment into sedimentary rock.

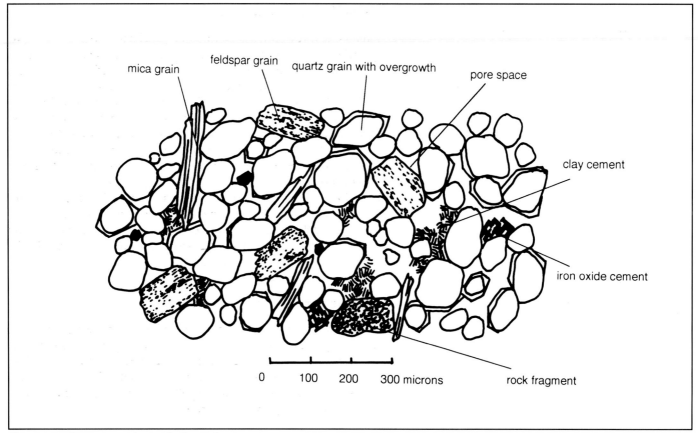

Figure 1.1 Structure of a typical sandstone.

Sandstone cements

It is the cement which, to a large extent, determines the weathering resistance of a sandstone. The cement holds a sandstone together by binding the mineral grains. The cement often does not completely fill the voids between grains but leaves gaps called pores which allow the free circulation of fluids within the sandstone. It is this porosity which can enhance the weathering rate of some sandstones. A rock such as granite, while it is mineralogically almost identical with some sandstones, has virtually no porosity and is more resistant to weathering. Any one sandstone can contain a number of different cements deposited at different times. It is rare for the pore space in a sandstone to be completely filled. Porosities in sandstones range from virtually zero up to about 30-35%. Values in the range 15-20% are common. A large variety of minerals may occur as cements.

Sandstones can be classified according to their cements:
Siliceous - Silica (quartz) cements.
Ferruginous - Iron oxide cements.
Argillaceous - Clay cements.
Calcareous - Calcite cements.
Dolomitic - Dolomite cements.

Siliceous sandstones are generally durable. These sandstones are cemented by silica (or quartz) which is deposited in the pore spaces of the rock leading to a very strongly bonded sandstone. Ferruginous sandstones owe their red colour to the iron oxide cements they contain. It takes only a very small amount (a few percent) of iron oxide to colour the stone and often the rock will contain other cement types (e.g. silica). Argillaceous sandstones often have very poor resistance to weathering. Calcareous and dolomitic cements are moderately resistant to natural weathering but are rapidly attacked by acidic water.

Classification of sandstones

Sandstones are defined as sedimentary rocks whose grain size is in the range 0.06 to 2 mm in diameter. Sandstones are classified on the basis of their mineralogy (Pettijohn, Potter and Siever, 1973). Sandstones contain variable amounts of fine-grained, silty (<30 μm ($^{30}/_{1000}$ mm)) matrix material. Those sandstones with >15% silty matrix are called wackes, those with less are termed arenites. Within each of these two groups the sandstones are subdivided according to the mineralogy of their constituent grains. The classification scheme is illustrated in a diagram where the three most common grain types:- quartz, feldspar and rock fragments, are plotted at the three vertices of a triangle (Figure 1.2). The vertices represent 100% of the particular component. All possible mixtures of these three components then plot inside the triangle. Within this classification, sandstones can be further sub-divided in terms of the cements they contain.

Colour variation in sandstones

Sandstones vary considerably in colour depending on their mineralogy. Pure quartz sandstones are white in colour. The presence of other minerals leads to colouration in the stone. Red sandstones contain iron oxides. Other iron containing minerals can give sandstone brown, orange or yellow colouration. The presence of clay causes grey and brown tints.

Sandstone quarrying

The number of operational sandstone quarries in Britain has decreased since the turn of the century. A survey by Leary (1986) found 58 still in production. The way stone is extracted is determined in part by the way in which the sandstone beds have been laid down. Several different methods of removing the stone from the bedding planes have be used. The aim is to extract from the quarry large rectangular blocks of stone, free from imperfections, which can then be cut and dressed as required.

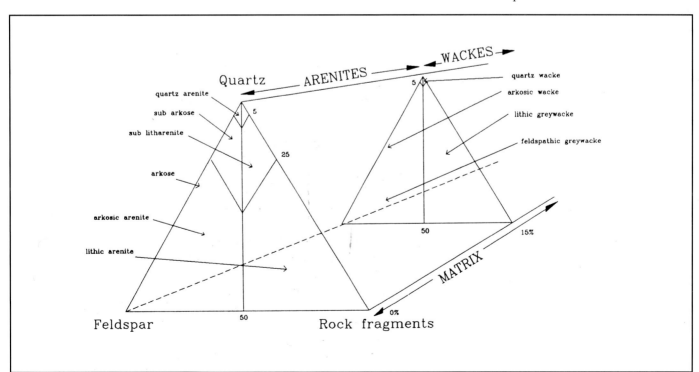

Figure 1.2 Classification scheme for sandstones (Pettijohn, Potter and Siever, 1973 and Greensmith, 1979).

Sandstone finishes

Sandstones used for construction purposes can have a variety of different finishes. The nature of the finish influences the way in which soiling is deposited on the surface, and hence the visual appearance of soiled sandstone buildings. On tooled surfaces, soiling tends to be deposited in a manner determined by the carved surface formed by the tooling instrument. The visual effect produced by soiling is influenced by the amount of soiling, the nature of the finish applied to the stone, and the way in which soiling has been deposited on the stone. The British Standard Institute (BS 5390) lists a number of surface finishes and pointing to stone. Commonly applied sandstone finishes include (Figure 1.3):

Polished	These surfaces are machined to give a smooth even finish, devoid of any tool marks. Polished finish can be left either matt or reflective.
Stugged	These finishes are hand worked using a pointed tool and mallet to produce small indentations over the entire surface.
Rockfaced	Produced by sharp blows to the edge of the stone using a pitching tool and hammer giving a natural rock faced appearance.
Droved	Hand or machine made shallow furrows are produced on the stone surface to give a regular, grooved finish to the stone.
Boasted	A range of regular patterns can be produced by the use of a pneumatic hand held chisel being heavily applied to the stone surface.

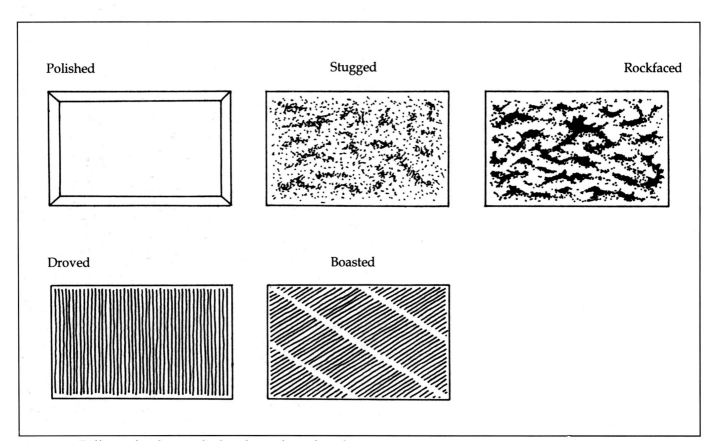

Figure 1.3 Different finishes applied to the surface of sandstones.

Bedding planes

Sandstones are laid down in beds, one on top of the other, forming a series of horizontal bedding planes. Wind and water currents which deposited the grains of sandstone can form localised diagonal cross-bedding patterns. Bedding patterns have important implications for the way in which stone is cut and used in buildings. When a stone is cut from the quarry face it is split along its natural bedding plane. In most situations the stone is laid according to its natural bed, so that pressure from the stone above it is perpendicular to the bedding plane. This gives the stone greater strength than if it is "face" or "edge" bedded where the bedding plane is placed vertically. A simple analogy can be made with the leaves of a book. If a book is laid flat, pressure can be applied from above without any ill effects. If the book is placed upright and pressure applied from above, the leaves bend, open out, and the book collapses. Pressure is acting along the bedding plane in face or edge bedded stone. This tends to force open the stone along its bedding plane, and cracks appear in the stone (Plate 1.1). Water can then travel more freely down vertical sections of the stone leading to spalling.

The builder, trying to produce a smooth outer surface on a wall with minimal tooling, may inadvertently bed the stone on face or edge in order to expose a smooth surface. This phenomenon is surprisingly common. With natural bedding, the height of the stone available is limited by the depth of the bedding planes in the quarry. In some situations the builder may have to use face or edge bedding for this reason, or to reduce the number of stones needed (and hence the number of joints) on free standing columns and mullions.

Plate 1.1 Cracks appearing in sandstone due to pressure acting through the bedding plane.

Chapter 2 The soiling of building facades

2.1 Building soiling

The soiling of building facades is a complex phenomenon which takes place at or near the surface of the stone and leads to a change in the appearance of the facade. This soiling can, for convenience, be sub-divided into two main groups, soiling caused by airborne particles and biological soiling due to the presence of microscopic flora. In practice, both types of soiling are likely to be present on stone surfaces, either separately or in combination. It is well recognised that soiling may be one cause of stone decay, leading to a loss of surface material. Alternatively, the soiling may take the form of surface discoloration which, although sometimes unsightly, need not necessarily result in damage to the stone surface.

Over the course of many decades of exposure to the elements, stones build up a patina on their surface which is not merely the accumulation of soiling material. Wetting and drying cycles cause mineralogical changes near the stone surface which, combined with external agencies such as soiling and pollutants, develop into a more or less stable surface zone of variable depth. Behind this patina, zones of varying mineralogical composition are often formed. Removal of this patina is not necessarily damaging to the stone in itself, but it is sometimes the case that a hard surface crust conceals underlying decay. Removal of the crust in such circumstances may result in serious damage to the stone, necessitating extensive replacement or repair. Colour changes may occur as a consequence of mobilisation of previously stable mineral assemblages under the surface of the stone. Re-establishment of the stable patina on a stone may take many years or decades.

Soiling does not occur in a uniform manner across the entire surface of a building. The nature of the surface material and the presence of architectural features, as well as micro-climatic effects, influence the water run-off patterns on the facade. These zones of water run-off, in addition to more protected areas (for example under projecting ledges) dictate the main areas of localised soiling, as well as, in some cases, creating localized areas of stone decay. In many instances the soiling over flat areas of facades is not uniform. Adjacent stones, apparently similar, can exhibit marked differences in soiling intensity. It is likely that this is influenced by the porosity, pore size distribution, capillary system, surface tension forces, and surface texture of the stone. These characteristics affect the absorption and evaporation of moisture in the stone. Little research work has been conducted on this phenomenon to date. From careful examination of the pattern of soiling on a building's facade, it is often possible to get some understanding of the reason why the building has soiled in the way it has. This understanding is important for two main reasons. Firstly, the distribution of soiling gives clues as to how the building is likely to be affected by cleaning. For example, areas subjected to frequent wetting which take longer to dry out, may remain discoloured following cleaning. In addition, the distribution of soiling gives some indication of the likely nature and pattern of resoiling following cleaning.

2.2 Non-biological soiling

Atmospheric constituents and pollutants

The atmosphere contains many types of pollutants, both naturally occurring, such as airborne soil particles, and many types of man-made pollutants, for example soot, industrial chemical emissions and vehicle exhaust emissions. Historically soot has been significant in respect to its soiling effect on building facades. Soiling may be visible on buildings after as little as one year's exposure to the atmosphere. Recent legislation has improved air quality, especially its optical quality, by reducing industrial emission of incomplete combustion products. Increasing vehicle exhaust emissions, which are soot to a large extent, continue to be important in facade soiling and stone decay. Brimblecome (1992) has documented the history of the accumulation and removal of soot deposits on buildings and legislation governing smoke abatement.

In modern urban atmospheres, oxides of sulphur and nitrogen are becoming more significant agents of stone decay, particularly for those stones containing calcite (calcium carbonate, $CaCO_3$) which include some sandstones. The way in which sulphur dioxide (SO_2) reacts in the atmosphere, and with building stone is well known. The sulphuric and sulphurous acids (H_2SO_4 and H_2SO_3 respectively) formed in the atmosphere transform stable calcite in the stone into calcium sulphate (gypsum, $CaSO_4.2H_2O$) which is moderately soluble in water. On areas of facades subject to run-off, gypsum does not accumulate on stone surfaces, rather it is washed off to expose fresh stone for further attack. On protected areas, such as under sills, the gypsum remains as a black crust. This is the classic process of deterioration of limestone. The formation of black gypsum crusts in sandstones is less well documented.

Aerosols

Aerosols are particles fine enough to be dispersed in the air and consist of particulates and gaseous pollutants. Particulate matter includes sulphates, nitrates, silicates, soot, and hydrocarbons. Contaminants include nitric acid (HNO_3), hydrochloric acid (HCl), sulphur trioxide (SO_3), nitrous oxides (NO_x), carbon dioxide (CO_2), hydrogen sulphide (H_2S) and ozone (O_3). Water in the form of an aerosol is very effective at reacting with atmospheric gases such as sulphur dioxide. In areas of high air pollution the acid formed can be quite concentrated.

Atmospheric aerosols vary in size from less than $0.1\mu m$ to larger than $2\mu m$. Particles in the 0.1-$2\mu m$ size range have the longest residence times in the atmosphere and can travel long distances before being deposited. Particles of this size include those formed by the coagulation of transient nuclei, (e.g. sulphates and nitrates). Soot and some organic matter (for example bacteria) can also be of a similar size. Larger particles ($>2\mu m$) are mainly terrestrial and are generally formed by mechanical processes (e.g. soil particles, sea salt, fly ash, bacteria, fungal spores, pollen and precipitation). These particles are transported by wind currents and, because of their mass, have only small residence times in the atmosphere and hence usually have only local effects on soiling (Verhoef, 1988).

Hicks (1982) describes the mechanisms of deposition of both wet and dry aerosol particles on sandstones. Wet deposition mainly takes the form of intermittent doses of pollutants, most of which are in dilute solution. The aerosols are formed by polluting material becoming incorporated into rain as it forms in cloud or by wash out during precipitation. Coarse particles due to their inertia, and fine particles, due to diffusion onto the surfaces of water droplets, are more easily incorporated into this deposition phase (Verhoef, 1988).

Dry deposition is a slower but more continuous process. It is greater on surfaces where condensation is taking place or where surfaces are wet. In these situations particles adhere to the moist surface of the stone. The particles remain attached to the surface when the moisture has evaporated. The rate of deposition of dry particles is closely related to air quality in the immediate vicinity of the stone. During the day, deposition tends to be greater on cooler surfaces.

The mechanisms of deposition of aerosols on stone surfaces are very complicated and are influenced by the physical and chemical nature of the stone.

Soot

Light absorbing particles, particularly soot, are important in terms of facade soiling. The level of soot present in the atmosphere tends to correlate with the degree of facade soiling, however it is probable that the attachment of soot particles has a low efficiency under wet conditions (Verhoef, 1988). Soot can fill the pore spaces of many sandstones (Schaffer, 1932). Heavy deposits of soot are commonly found on areas of sloping facades (for example on window ledges). The soiling patterns found on facades are typically the result of the eroding effect, water run-off and soot deposits on the surface of the stone (Verhoef, 1988).

2.3 Atmospheric factors influencing soiling

Water

Mist in the air causes coagulation of particles and hence their sedimentation. Rain and other forms of atmospheric water can capture particles and atmospheric pollutants and precipitate them. The concentration of these pollutants is increased in foggy weather, when coagulation of the particles takes place.

Surface condensation on the face of stone contributes to the soiling of the surface. Winter conditions in Scotland typically produce an ambient relative humidity in excess of 80%, and promote condensation on the stone surface. It may therefore be surmised that the geographical location of the building and its micro-climate will exert a considerable influence on the rate of soiling and decay of the stone.

Temperature

The high thermal capacity of stone on external surfaces has the effect of creating a temperature gradient within the boundary layer of air in contact with the stone. The surface temperature of the stone may be significantly below that of the ambient air. As there is more molecular agitation in hot air than in cold air, there is a tendency for dust to be condensed onto the colder surface (Verhoef, 1988).

Wind and micro-climate effects

Wind flow patterns around buildings are complex, being influenced by the site topography and architectural features, resulting in fluctuating zones of suction and pressure and local vortices and turbulence. It has been noted that, under light wind conditions (i.e. minimum turbulence), particles tend to be deposited on windward faces. In stronger wind conditions the increased negative pressures and eddies on leeward faces will tend to concentrate dirt in these locations (Verhoef, 1988). Plate 2.1 gives an example of the way in which micro-climate, particularly prevailing wind and rain direction, influences soiling distribution.

Rainwater run-off

The architectural features and the fenestration of elevations of buildings and monuments have a direct influence on soiling, due principally to the rainfall run-off patterns on the facade. On most buildings the rainfall run-off is usually vertical, although local features may cause diversions to the water flow path, breaking the stream into flows with relatively fixed directions.

Rainfall mainly strikes the top part of an external wall and produces a run-off film down the wall which is a few tenths of a millimetre in thickness (Verhoef, 1988). Projecting elements may provide some shelter from water run-off. A feature of sandstone buildings in particular is the heavily soiled zone below large glazed areas. These areas are subjected to the greater volumes of water run-off from glazed areas. With limestones, water run-off from horizontal or sloping surfaces produces a clean washed zone immediately below the feature followed, at a lower level, by a more heavily soiled zone. This is due to dirt, transported from above, being redeposited on the drier surface at a lower level (Verhoef, 1988).

Soiling caused by rainwater run-off can be reduced by the insertion of thin metal strips into the mortar of projecting stonework (Plate 2.2). These strips redirect the rainwater run-off directly to the ground and away from the stonework below the strips.

2.4 Fluid movement and surface changes

Fluid movements

Fluids may move within porous stone with considerable ease. Water gains access to the interior of the stone through exposed faces and by transfer from the surrounding stones and mortar joints. The direction of these fluid movements can change as a result of changes in atmospheric conditions (temperature and humidity). Pore fluids can be drawn to exposed surfaces where evaporation at, or adjacent to, the surface takes place. Minerals from within the stone may be taken into solution and re-precipitated at or near the surface. This natural precipitation of dissolved minerals contributes to the formation of surface crusts or patinas.

Water is the single most important factor in the decay of stone. Processes which hinder the evaporation of water from the sandstone surface or increase throughput of water can potentially lead to accelerated stone decay. Soiling has the effect of blocking spaces between the sandstone particles on or near the surface of the stone. This in turn reduces surface permeability, restricting the movement of water both into and out of the stone. Heavy build-up of soiling at the stone surface can therefore act to prevent water loss from the stone and may accelerate decay. However, if the soiling layer is permeable to water vapour, moisture will still be able to escape from the stone, and, due to reduced water ingression rates through the low permeability surface layer, rates of decay may be lower on the soiled stone.

It is not clear if any generalisation can be made regarding whether soiling increases or decreases the rate of decay of sandstone. It is likely that the effects differ depending on the nature of the sandstone and the characteristics of the soiling layer. It is generally agreed that the thick crusts of calcium sulphate which are found on limestones are detrimental to the stone. The situation is less clear with respect to the effects of soiling on sandstone and granite.

Many sedimentary rocks such as sandstones and limestones have quite high porosities and are capable of absorbing relatively large volumes of water by capillary and other processes. Other stone types such as granites have virtually no porosity and absorb little or no water if they are undamaged.

Plate 2.1 Micro-climatic effects have influenced the pattern of soiling on this stone.

Plate 2.2 Thin metal strips inserted into the mortar of projecting stonework to redirect water run-off away from stonework below.

Iron staining of sandstones

Analysis of surface soiling on sandstones will often indicate the presence of iron oxides and hydroxides which have migrated from within the stone. Fluid movement within the body of a sandstone over many years dissolves and alters minerals and may re-precipitate them on, or close to, the surface of the stone as evaporation takes place. If the minerals leached from within the stone are dark coloured (such as those containing iron and manganese) their redeposition at the surface can cause aesthetically displeasing staining. This type of staining occurs naturally. When buildings are cleaned this staining can become more noticeable. Sometimes this naturally occuring staining revealed after cleaning, is mistakenly thought to have been caused in the cleaning process. The degree to which weathering and soiling affect individual sandstones depends on their mineralogy. In some cases removal of iron-rich minerals from the outermost millimetres of the stone by weathering can leave the stone surface a lighter colour.

Iron staining can also be caused by the action of stone cleaning chemicals. Staining occurs in a similar way to "natural" iron staining, by the leaching of coloured minerals within the sandstone and their re-precipitation at the surface. However, in this case large amounts of these minerals (mainly iron) are mobilised over a short period. If this mobilised iron is then removed by stone cleaning, it can result in a "bleached" stone surface.

Sandstones in contact with other materials

The rate at which sandstones decay and soil can be influenced by other materials with which they are in contact. Snethlage (1985) reports a mechanism which would seem to account for the increased staining and deterioration sometimes found when sandstone is in contact with less porous (denser) material such as granite plinths or dense mortar joints. He suggests that rain water flowing down a facade is soaked up more by the porous stone, or concentrated in the bottom of stones where further downward moisture movement is restricted by less permeable material. The aggressive components of rain water, salts and acids, are concentrated at the contact zones between the porous sandstone and other less porous materials. This creates a moisture gradient in the lower levels of the sandstone with an increased moisture content at the lowest level. Moisture will evaporate from the stone surface and there will be a zone in which the rate of supply of moisture to the surface by capillary and other forces is balanced by the rate of evaporation. Salt solutions are concentrated at the surface extremities of the zone, resulting in the "tide-mark" of salts which is commonly seen. Moisture movement in these zones can lead to increased soiling, enhanced salt efflorescences and increased strain on the contact zones of porous stone, resulting in greater damage to the stone in these areas.

2.5 Other non-biological contaminants

Paint

The visual appearance of cleaned buildings can be marred by paint deposits on stone. Ashurst & Ashurst (1988) suggest that paint can sometimes be removed from masonry by methylene chloride (paint stripper) applied as a poultice under a plastic film. Proprietary poultice paint strippers, based on caustic soda (sodium hydroxide), are also available. Once applied to the paint the poultice is left to dry before being lifted off. The masonry is then thoroughly washed down. It should be stressed that the effect which these treatments have on different stone surfaces has not been fully researched. Extreme caution should be exercised before any of these treatments are contemplated. Application of some of the chemicals used in these paint removers could be very damaging to stone.

Aerosol paint (graffiti)

Cleaned masonry may be more susceptible to graffiti attack than heavily soiled stone. While most aerosol based paints can be removed from the stone surface, problems can arise when pigments are carried into the pores by solvents in the paint. The application of solvents to remove the paint can sometimes result in the pigments being driven more deeply into the stone. Ashurst & Ashurst (1988) lists a number of chemicals available to remove aerosol paints including water-rinsable paint strippers, 1:5 solutions of water and trisodium phosphate, and sodium hydroxide poultices. Chemical strippers are applied to the affected surface for a period of time sufficient to allow the paint to soften. The paint is then removed by brushing or scraping. After removal of the paint the masonry must be thoroughly washed (Ashurst & Ashurst , 1988).

As indicated with paint removing chemicals, it should be stressed that the effect which aerosol paint removal treatments have on stone surfaces is not fully understood. Extreme caution should be exercised before any of these treatments are contemplated. More aggressive treatments should only be used when less aggressive methods have failed. Removal of aerosol paints can result in patches on the masonry, particularly if the treatment is carried out on a number of occasions. Very low pressure grit blasting, using a pencil jet and aluminium oxide as an abrasive can also be used to remove graffiti. Visual problems can sometimes arise with "ghosting" effects remaining on the stone following physical methods of graffiti removal.

A number of anti-graffiti treatments are commercially available. These work by forming a barrier to prevent the migration of paint into the stone. These treatments are sometimes claimed to allow the removal of paint to be achieved quickly, without the use of caustic strippers. Before application of any barrier treatment, the possible effects on the stone must be investigated. This would include any changes the treatment had on stone colour and water permeability. Barrier treatments should not be used on decaying stone. Ashurst & Ashurst (1988) suggests in these cases alkoxysilane treatments, which penetrate deeper into the stone might be used. Anti-graffiti treatments have only a limited effective life, possibly less than five years (Ashurst & Ashurst , 1988). The problem of graffiti is currently being investigated at the Building Research Establishment (BRE).

2.6 Biological soiling

Algae

Algal growths are usually green when fresh, becoming black when the surface dries out. Most algae which colonise stone belong to the class of green algae. Colours other than green may occur, depending on the species present. Red, brown and blue-green species of algae are common. They appear slimy if the surface is moist. They are very common on the exterior surfaces of buildings and can be found on almost any substrate which remains damp for long enough. Algae are photosynthetic and require light to grow. They may die or become inactive during a prolonged dry spell but spores and propagules left on the stone will regenerate when the surface is rewetted.

Opinion is divided as to whether algae in themselves are capable of causing stone degradation. Algae are an indication of persistent damp conditions. They may increase susceptibility to damage caused by long term water retention.

Fungi

These include "moulds" and "mildews". They are not photosynthetic and do not require light to grow but they require organic material as a food source. They may be grey, green, black or brown in colour and often take the form of furry spots or patches on the surface of the substrate (BRE, 1982).

Some fungi secrete organic acids as they grow. These include oxalic, citric, acetic acids and many more. These are capable of dissolving mineral grains. Although fungal secretions are capable of dissolving minerals in stone, they are unlikely in most circumstances to cause serious damage to the stone substrate, although they can cause disfiguring staining. The mechanical activity of hyphal growth can also contribute to stone decay (Koestler *et al.*, 1985).

Bacteria

There are many different forms of bacteria but all are too small to be visible to the naked eye. Some are capable of fixing nitrogen from the atmosphere and can therefore aid the colonisation of a substrate by other organisms through increased availability of nitrogen. They are able to resist extremes of temperature and drought. Secretions of both organic and inorganic acids can cause erosion of stone.

Sulphur oxidising bacteria can be damaging to vulnerable stone types, such as those containing carbonate minerals (e.g. limestone), through the production of sulphuric acid. Biologically produced gypsum has been found on marble and is associated with sulphur oxidising bacteria such as *Thiobacillus sp.* (Sramek, 1980).

Lichens

Lichens are a symbiotic intergrowth of algae and fungi. They are photosynthetic organisms which require light and mineral salts for growth. They are often grey, yellow or orange in colour. Some of the body of the lichen may penetrate into the surface of the substrate. The lichen thallus can penetrate deeply into the stone releasing organic acids which can damage stone. Deposits of oxalates may be formed at the lichen/stone interface. Oxalates deposited below the surface (particularly in microporous stone) can restrict the ability of a stone to "breathe" leading to damage by surface spalling (Richardson, 1991). Lichens are very slow growing and in most cases appear to cause little or no damage to stone surfaces. The mosaic of different coloured lichens on the stone may be considered to have a pleasing effect. However, in some cases lichens can cause blistering and spalling on stone surfaces (Plate 2.3).

2.7 Conditions needed for colonisation

The conditions required for organic growths to occur vary depending on the type and species of organism. Photosynthetic organisms can survive with moisture, mineral salts and light. Other organisms require moisture and an organic substrate but not light. Many organisms can withstand severe dehydration for long periods but active growth usually requires relatively high moisture levels in the stone or high humidity. The main factors influencing development of micro-organisms on a surface are water, light, temperature, pH and nutrition.

Water

The availability of water is probably the most critical factor in allowing the colonisation of a stone surface, and the amount of water determines the species of organisms which occur. Different moisture levels in the same stone type often support different biological communities (Agarossi *et al.*, 1985; Danin and Caneva, 1990). The duration of dampness is more important than the frequency of wetting (Bravery and Jones, 1977; Grant, 1982). Organic growths themselves inhibit drying of the surface and affect the moisture retention properties of the surfaces they colonise (Bravery, 1982).

Light

Photosynthetic organisms such as algae require light to grow. Some non-photosynthetic organisms can be killed by excessive light.

Temperature

Species vary in their sensitivity to temperature. In general, most biological growths are fairly tochanges in temperature of the range found on external substrate. For every species there is an optimum temperature for growth and maximum and minimum temperatures outside which growth ceases. However, the spores of many species can survive for long periods in extremes of temperature (Verhoef, 1988).

pH

The pH is measured on a scale of 1-14. A neutral medium (such as distilled water) has a pH value of 7. Numbers below 7 indicate relative acidity, numbers above 7 indicate relative alkalinity. Micro-organisms vary in their sensitivity to pH. Some can only tolerate a narrow range, others are more tolerant and can flourish over a wide range of pH. Highly alkaline substrates, above pH 9 are unsuitable for algal colonisation (Grant, 1982).

Nutrition

There is a progression or cycle of species involved in the colonisation of stone. The order of colonisation is principally controlled by the availability of nutrients and moisture. This situation arises because fresh stone has little in the way of available nutrients for organisms. The initial colonisers of the stone are organisms such as algae and some bacteria which do not require organic nutrients in order to grow. Once such colonies have become established, accumulation of organic matter can lead to further colonisation by other organisms such as fungi, mosses and higher plants.

2.8 Algal growth on building facades

On building facades green algal assemblages are the predominant form of biological soiling and colonise a wide range of substrates including stone and mortar joints. They are often well developed on wall surfaces subjected to excessive water run-off from leaking gutters and downpipes.

Several factors may account for the differences in the time of appearance of algae on stone surfaces. The most significant factor is the dampness of the surface, which is principally influenced by exposure to water and the porosity of the stone (Plate 2.4). The inclination and orientation of the surface are also important factors governing algal growth. The nature of the surface is also influential, rough surfaces tending to encourage algal growth when compared to smoother surfaces.

A simple experiment (Webster *et al.*, 1992) exposing an uncontaminated plate of smooth Clashach sandstone, inclined at an angle of 70° with a south orientation, showed evidence of colonisation by green algae after six months exposure in the north east of Scotland over a period September to February. Twelve months exposure resulted in almost complete colonisation of the top surface of the plate. The underside was also exposed to the atmosphere but was not colonised. During the drier summer period growth ceased and the colour changed to dark brown or black. In autumn and winter with increased precipitation and reduced solar radiation active growth quickly restarted, with accompanying return of the green coloration.

Algae produce small amounts of organic acids which could potentially dissolve stone components. The main contribution algae appear to make to stone weathering is through the physical action of wet/dry and freeze/thaw cycles of muciliage and the growths themselves. They would therefore appear capable of changing the physical characteristics of the stone surface by altering capillary diameters, and the size of very small fissures. Decay of stone surfaces by algae is not thought to be significant when set against chemical and physical weathering phenomena. Nevertheless, the presence of algae on surfaces encourages water entrapment and reduced rates of drying which may exacerbate water-induced damage to the substrate (Bravery, 1982).

Algae also affect the aesthetic characteristics of the building. Algae tend to trap soot and other particulates giving the surface a darkened, dirty appearance. Also, as the habitat becomes less favourable for algal growth due to increased levels of surface pollution, the growth itself can become dark coloured.

As urban atmospheric pollution levels continue to change it is likely that increased biological soiling will take place containing a wider range of subaerial flora than is presently found in towns and cities.

There is a surprising lack of information available on this important aspect of facade soiling. An excellent review paper (John, 1988) provides a most comprehensive coverage of algal growth on buildings.

2.9 Removal of biological organisms

There are a large number of situations where biological growths do no structural damage to masonry and where their removal seems pointless. Indeed in many circumstances biological growths (in particular lichens) can enhance the aesthetic appeal of buildings. The growth of lichens on roof tiles, for example, is considered appealing by some.

A range of methods is available for the removal of organisms. The main treatment involves the use of biocides.

Biocides

There are a number of factors which must be taken into account when considering the use of biocides. The treatment must be able to kill the problem organisms whilst causing no harm to other living organisms or damage to the stone itself. The treatment should have a reasonably long effective life. The effective life of biocides varies depending on the nature and concentration of the treatment, the nature of the substrate and the exposure of the treated area. Sheltered areas of porous stone will be protected for longer than exposed areas of low porosity (BRE, 1992). Ideally the biocidal treatment should not leave deposits in the stone, alter the natural stone colour or affect the structure of the stone in ways which could lead to, or exacerbate, long term damage (Richardson, 1973; 1975). If the biocide treatment leaves salts in the stone for instance, efflorescences may occur which can lead to spalling of the stone surface. Alteration or acceleration of the natural weathering cycle of the stone may result if the treatment causes changes to the near surface porosity of the stone, altering its moisture absorption and evaporation properties. Some compounds, such as phenols, can cause colour changes by reaction with iron in the substrate or the components of the stone itself (BRE, 1992; Richardson, 1973).

Biocides should be applied during a period of dry weather, to ensure that the biocide has time to kill the organisms before it is washed out of the stone (BRE, 1992). Where the stone is heavily infested with growth, removal of some organic material, by brushing, prior to application of the biocide will help. The biocide should be well brushed in (BRE, 1992). Alternatively, pneumatic garden-type sprayers can be used (Ashurst, 1988). After the initial application and brushing to get rid of dead matter, a reapplication of the biocide may be necessary since much of the biocide may have been absorbed by the organisms (Richardson, 1973).

Some organisms such as lichens resist wetting after a long dry spell. It may, in such cases, be necessary to prewet the surface to assist absorption of the biocide by the organisms (BRE, 1992).

Organisms vary widely in their susceptibility to biocides. A treatment which can effectively kill one species of microorganism may leave another completely unaffected.

Reference should be made to the relevant health and safety regulations before the start of any biocide treatment.

Other methods of biological control

It is possible to remove some organisms, including algae, lichens and mosses, by scraping or brushing with non wire brushes followed by washing down with water. However, the stone may retain "ring marks" from lichens and micro-organisms. These can rapidly regenerate themselves from spores or, in the case of lichens, from the thallus underlying the stone surface.

Water repellents have been used to prevent growth on porous stone. However, established growth should be removed by application of a biocide and brushing prior to treatment (Richardson, 1973). In some cases the use of water repellents is inadvisable. This is the case where the stone may be subject to wetting from an internal source, for instance, by rising damp or water seepage through the wall interior or joints. If this moisture is unable to evaporate normally, it will almost certainly cause spalling of the treated surface either by freezing damage or by salt deposition (Richardson, 1973).

Building design and biological growths

Building design affects both the likelihood of colonisation by organisms and the effective life of preventative treatments. Biological growths predominate on horizontal and sloping surfaces, particularly those having a northerly aspect. Any structures which project above roof level, or project beyond the facade are particularly vulnerable to algal colonisation. Sheltered surfaces due to their lower moisture content are less likely to be colonised by organisms and, if they are not washed by rain water, any biocidal treatment will remain in the stone for a longer period.

Biological growth can be limited by designs which provide areas protected from direct rainfall and which shed water quickly .

Plate 2.3 Lichen causing blistering and decay on a stone surface.

Plate 2.4 Algae growing on sandstone and granite surfaces. Algal growth is greater on sandstone than on granite due to the higher porosity of the sandstone.

23

Chapter 3   Stonecleaning aesthetics

3.1 Aesthetic considerations

Buildings are cleaned for a variety of reasons, one of the main being for the visual, perceptual and aesthetic improvements which are thought to result from cleaning. Clearly, the cleaning of heavily soiled buildings not only changes their appearance in fundamental ways, but has a marked effect on the way surrounding buildings are perceived. In recent years the assumption that cleaning is always beneficial in terms of environmental aesthetic improvements has been brought into question.

The urban planner and cleaning practitioner needs to address a number of issues relating to environmental aesthetics before any decisions are taken about cleaning. These issues range from macro concerns at the townscape and neighbourhood level through to the micro level of individual stones which make up the building facade. Only after full consideration of the likely aesthetic implications, should a programme of cleaning be undertaken. While it is not possible to predict in advance precisely what the visual and perceptual outcome of cleaning will be, many past mistakes could have been avoided by more careful consideration of the aesthetic consequences prior to the commencement of cleaning.

Townscapes

Urban planners have, as a central concern, the unity of the urban environment. In many urban situations a unity exists between buildings and between streets which gives an identity to whole areas of cities. In some situations, particularly those where buildings are constructed of similar material, the uniformity of soiling across a whole district might add to the sense of place of the region, distinguishing it from its neighbours. Some good examples of where this unity appears to operate are selected areas of Edinburgh New Town, where stonecleaning in some streets has been restricted. The result has been that the area has retained a degree of uniformity (Plate 3.1). In other urban areas, uniformity may be achieved by widespread cleaning activity while at the same time adding to a sense of urban renewal. It is important, before decisions about cleaning are made, for planners to survey the urban fabric, recording the nature and extent of the soiling in an area, so as to guide overall stonecleaning policy in the region.

A further issue which concerns urban planners, and which stonecleaning has a direct bearing on, is the concept of imageability. This can be seen as the ability of environmental stimuli to evoke images in the minds of observers. The concept derives from the work of Lynch (1960), who suggests that urban images are composed of five elements: paths, edges, nodes, landmarks and districts. This might provide a framework from which stonecleaning policy could be developed. Other writers (e.g. Cullen, 1961) have addressed questions of the aesthetic feel of urban environments, stressing issues such as congruity, complexity, mystery and surprise, concepts on which building soiling and stonecleaning have a direct bearing.

Plate 3.1 Edinburgh (New Town district). The unity of this district has been maintained by restrictions on cleaning.

Streetscapes

In the past some of the worst damage in terms of the detrimental visual effects of stonecleaning has been to streetscapes. The problem in essence stems from owners of individual properties in terraces, circles, crescents and squares cleaning their properties in isolation (Plate 3.2). These architectural forms were built with unity of storey height, fenestration, detailing and building material and were clearly designed to be read as a whole. If only some of these buildings are cleaned, this unity is invariably destroyed (Plate 3.3). While this piecemeal approach may encourage other owners to clean their properties, this argument presupposes that wholesale cleaning is advantageous, a view which, in itself, is open to question. Also, this type of cleaning policy has the considerable disadvantage that the result of cleaning adjacent buildings at different times, invariably leads to differences in stone colour and texture. Individual properties in terraces, cleaned over an extended period, enter the resoiling cycle at different times. The problem is made much worse when different methods of cleaning are employed on the same street (Plate 3.4). Where care is taken to clean terraces as a complete unit the results are much more aesthetically pleasing (Plate 3.5). In narrow streets, which have tall buildings on either side, stonecleaning can result in greater amounts of reflected light reaching street level, reducing the oppressive nature of tall, heavily soiled buildings. This may be particularly welcome in residential areas (Plate 3.6). In short, if a decision to clean in a street is made, cleaning must take place at the same time using the same method over the entire street facade. Andrew and Crawford (1992) give a review of conservation and planning considerations in relation to stonecleaning.

Plate 3.2 The cleaning of the single facade has compromised the unity of this terrace.

Plate 3.3 Piecemeal cleaning of terraces inevitably produces poor aesthetic results.

Plate 3.4 15-21 Park Circus, Glasgow. The properties in this crescent have been cleaned on an individual basis. The result is not as pleasing as 22-29 Park Circus which was cleaned as a single unit (Plate 3.5).

Plate 3.5 22-29 Park Circus, Glasgow. This crescent has been cleaned as a single unit.

Plate 3.6 The cleaning of these tenements has resulted in a marked increase in reflected light at street level.

Architectural detail

The removal of soiling can help reveal architectural features (Plates 3.7 & 3.8). Cleaning can also have the effect of removing details and sharp edges from stone (Plates 3.9 & 3.10). The potential damage to architectural detail needs to be considered before decisions about cleaning are made.

Plate 3.7 Before cleaning.
Area of soiled detail showing obscuration of features.

Plate 3.8 After cleaning.
Much improved contrast after cleaning helps reveal sculptured details.

Plate 3.9 Before cleaning.
Note sharpness of stone detail.

Plate 3.10 After cleaning.
Loss of sharp detailing is apparent.

Staining

Staining arises from a variety of different causes and can be aesthetically detrimental to the appearance of cleaned buildings. Water stains in particular are often partly hidden by soiling and only become noticeable when the building is cleaned. Often, careful examination of the soiled facade of a building will reveal where underlying staining is already present. Some indication of the likely visual end result, in terms of staining, can sometimes be made prior to cleaning (Plate 3.11). In some cases stonecleaning may reveal the extent and cause of staining and stone decay and allow for repairs to be more easily made. Much of the staining (and stone decay) revealed by stonecleaning is the result of poor building maintenance and neglect of guttering and downpipes. Decisions about the acceptability, and what, if anything, can or should be done to ameliorate the detrimental aesthetic effects of any revealed staining, needs to be considered prior to any cleaning.

Orange staining, particularly on sandstone buildings, indicates the presence of iron oxides. As indicated in Chapter 2 this staining can result from natural processes occurring within the stone or be the result of chemical stonecleaning. As with water staining, stonecleaning tends to make iron staining from whatever cause more noticeable (Plate 3.12 & 3.13).

Plate 3.11 Part of a partially cleaned sandstone terrace.

Note the very visible water staining on the upper left hand corner of the cleaned facade. This staining extends to, and can be detected in, the soiled layer of the adjacent facade. Cleaning has made the stain more visible. A careful inspection of the building prior to cleaning would have revealed the areas affected by water staining and given some indication of the likely end result of cleaning. Note also the aesthetically detrimental water staining which has been revealed along the parapet. In addition, the unity of the terrace has been adversely affected by its partial cleaning.

Plate 3.12 Soiled ashlar sandstone before cleaning. Note how soiling tends to obscure stains and small blemishes on the masonry surface.

Plate 3.13 After cleaning (same area as shown above). Stains and blemishes on the stonework are much more apparent following cleaning.

Colour

Stonecleaning produces dramatic changes to the colour of buildings. The stonecleaning method adopted, and its application have critical effects on the colour of stone. Evidence of the large scale variations in colour produced by different cleaning methods can be seen in situations where an individual stone on a facade has been subjected to different stonecleaning techniques (Plate 3.14). The problem can be further compounded by any time lag between treatments. The colour of stonework following cleaning has been shown to have important implications for the aesthetic judgement of buildings (Webster *et al.*,1992).

The quite dramatic changes in the colour of stone which are sometimes observed in the field, after chemical cleaning, should not normally occur. The most likely reason for colour changes are errors in the chemical cleaning regime applied. Before any choice of cleaning system is made, sample panels should be checked for colour differentials. Portable electronic colour monitoring equipment is available for the accurate measurement of stone colour.

Plate 3.14 Differences in the colour of individual stones in a facade can be detected after having been cleaned by two different methods.

Indenting stone

The question of indentation of new stone in soiled facades and whether this necessitates the cleaning of the whole facade is often raised in connection with stonecleaning. Indentation, in itself, very rarely provides sufficient reason to clean. It is common practise to indent historic buildings without cleaning. Situations where the stone is not heavily soiled, or where there is little colour variation between original stonework and indents, or where the original stonework is patchy and of different stone types are situations where indents provide least visual distraction. The nature of the architectural feature being indented also has a bearing on appearance. In order that new stone does not disrupt the aesthetics of the facade, it may be worth considering replacing specific elements such as string courses, dressings, mouldings or rybats in their entirety to maintain the unity of form and symmetry, although in historic building and other buildings where the aim is to conserve as much of the original fabric as possible, this course of action may be out of the question. Indenting can be visually problematic where there is a high proportion of new stone or where the rhythm of the facade is disrupted by indents. However, indents do blend in relatively quickly (Plate 3.15). Indented stone can be given a light covering of solutions of soot or other inert material to tone down the new stone. Where buildings are cleaned care should be taken to ensure that indented stone is of a similar colour, texture, nature and where possible from the same quarry as surrounding stone (Plate 3.16). Ashurst (1988) gives extensive guidance on the repair and replacement of stone.

Plate 3.15 After a few years indents blend in with soiled stone.

Plate 3.16 Indented stone cut to match the original.

34

3.2 Stonecleaning case studies

The relationship between soiling and a building's aesthetic quality is complex. It is clear from research evidence (Webster *et al.*, 1992) that heavily soiled buildings can benefit aesthetically from cleaning. The improvement in visual quality is dependent on a range of factors, two important considerations being the type and application of the stonecleaning method employed and the condition of the masonry being cleaned. Case study examples of different stonecleaned buildings reveal the range in quality of finish often found with stonecleaning work.

Case study 1

Plates 3.17 and 3.18 show similar sandstone facades, one of which has been cleaned. The soiled facade appears dark and unattractive. The colour of the stonework and its architectural features such as window surrounds and stone carvings are obscured by soiling. In comparison, the cleaned facade is brighter and less depressing visually. Its architectural features are more discernible. The symmetry of the facade is once again apparent. In effect the building has been restored to more closely resemble its original appearance. Whether these are valid reasons to clean old buildings is open to question.

Plate 3.17 Soiled sandstone facade.

Plate 3.18 Cleaned sandstone facade.

Case study 2

Plate 3.19 shows part of a row of Glasgow tenements which have been cleaned. The contrast between the soiled and cleaned properties is very marked. Cleaning of the whole street, using the same method at the same time would have avoided the contrast. If the soiled tenements are eventually cleaned it will be very difficult to obtain unity of colour. However, the tenement itself has been cleaned as a complete unit.

Cleaning has revealed heavy iron staining (resulting from natural weathering processes) on some stones, which detracts from the visual appeal of the total facade. The opportunity to replace windows and doors is often taken while scaffolding is in place for stone repairs or stonecleaning. Note also how new windows have added to the change in overall appearance. All too often replacements by inappropriate windows and doors detract from the overall appearance.

Plate 3.19 Stonecleaning in a residential street.

Case study 3

Plate 3.20 shows Kelvingrove Art Gallery, Glasgow. Cleaning has enhanced the appearance of this building. Its setting within a park, devoid of buildings in the immediate vicinity, avoids the problem of cleaned buildings contrasting with nearby soiled ones.

Plate 3.20 Kelvingrove Art Gallery, Glasgow.

Case study 4

Plate 3.21 shows an Edinburgh building where only the ground floor has been cleaned. The effect of this has been to highlight the soiled stone above and to have an adverse affect on streetscaping. Cleaning in this piecemeal fashion should be avoided. Note the residual soiling around the base of the ground floor windows caused by water run-off from sills.

Plate 3.21 The detrimental aesthetic effects caused by the partial cleaning of a building.

3.3 Aesthetics and soiling

Building facades pass through cycles of change as soiling accumulates on the exterior surface. The speed of this change varies considerably. Materials vary in their susceptibility to the influence of weathering, but every material, and so every facade, alters in appearance after long exposure to atmospheric pollution, wind and rain. Many modern buildings, for example those with exposed precast concrete exteriors or harled surfaces, quickly develop patterns of staining through rainwater run-off which are unrelated to any underlying architectural feature and may look unkempt after only a few years (Plate 3.22).

Many old buildings which have developed accumulations of soiling over long periods of time may display an aesthetic quality which enhances the appeal of the building. Indeed, the expectation of some buildings are that they will be soiled. An example of this is Edinburgh Castle (Plate 3.23), which has a considerable accumulation of soiling on its facades. Research (Webster *et al.*, 1992) has shown that the perception of its character would be lost if this soiling was removed. This phenomenon may well extend to other old buildings.

Plate 3.22 Although this building is only lightly soiled it already looks unkempt.

Plate 3.23 Edinburgh Castle.
Soiling is part of its character and aids the perception of the age of the castle.

Facade complexity and soiling

Soiling on buildings which is either consonant with the underlying texture of the building facade or enhances architectural details can, within certain limits, enhance the aesthetic appeal of buildings. Conversely, soiling which is dissonant with the underlying texture of a building (e.g. heavy soiling which obscures colour) or which is unrelated to the building's architecture is aesthetically displeasing. Many modern buildings are constructed of materials, or are of designs, which do not allow for consonant weathering and soiling patterns. When soiled, they are visually less acceptable than older buildings which, through the materials used or design features, allow for longer periods of consonant weathering.

Soiling changes the perception of facades and can be seen to progress through a sequence, with facade cleaning interrupting this progression and returning the building to an earlier stage in the cycle. Initially, light soiling on surfaces which have an uneven texture (e.g. rock faced and tooled stone) lodges mainly on horizontal and outermost surfaces of the stone. Similarly, light soiling around architectural detail adds to the visual complexity of the building by increasing contrast and shadowing effects. Verhoef (1988) argues that in northerly cities of Europe, soiling can emphasise architectural designs which for much of the year would be lacking definition due to the absence of sharp, well defined shadows.

Moderate soiling of building facades can result in a change in the visual appearance of buildings which has an interactional effect with the underlying architectural features or stone surface. This type of soiling changes the visual complexity of the building by obscuring some detail, colour and texture, while at the same time adding a pattern of soiling which was originally absent (Plate 3.24). This interactional effect differs with stone type. On rock faced and tooled surfaces a heavier build up of soiling may be more acceptable aesthetically thanit would be on smooth or polished stonework. While initially soiling may be related to the underlying architectural surface (for example in bedding planes, Plate 3.25), patterns of soiling eventually arise which are unrelated to the underlying detail.

Continued soiling eventually leads to a complete blackening of the surface of the building which reduces the visual information of architectural details and completely obscures the colour, texture and any shadowing effects. In effect the visual complexity of the building is reduced by the very heavy soiling on the building facade.

Entire buildings may progress through this pattern of light to heavy soiling in a relatively consistent way. Alternatively, parts of facades may soil at different rates (Plate 3.26).

Plate 3.24 Soiling on rock faced stone.
A low level of soiling can add to the visual complexity of a building and is not necessarily aesthetically detrimental.

Plate 3.25 Soiling in these bedding planes is aesthetically acceptable and may enhance the appearance of the stone.

Plate 3.26 This building has soiled at different rates across its facade. The upper gable end is heavily soiled, obscuring stone colour and detail. Lower sections of the building are less heavily soiled and are aesthetically more pleasing.

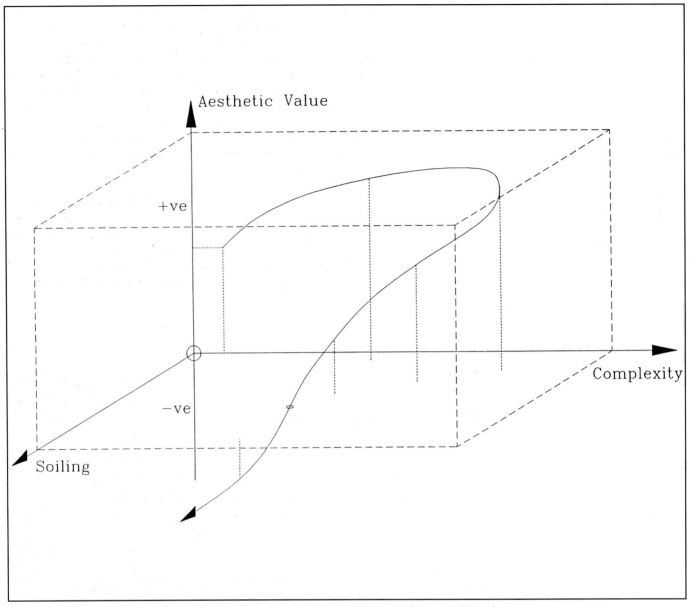

Figure 3.1 A model of the relationship between soiling, building complexity and aesthetics.

The cycle of sandstone building weathering suggests that soiling affects building complexity and aesthetics in a relationship shown by Figure 3.1. The shape of this graph may vary considerably due to many factors among which are type and age of building and materials used in construction. Figure 3.1 may be seen hypothetically to represent the weathering pattern of many tooled, rock faced and rubble stone buildings. On some buildings various parts of the facade may be at different points on the graph. For example in Plate 3.26 parts of the facade with lower levels of soiling and a higher level of complexity, for instance those areas towards the base of the building, are at a point nearer to the maximum aesthetic value. Those parts of the facade with heavier soiling and thus reduced complexity, for instance the upper parts of the building, are aesthetically less pleasing and thus at a lower point on the graph. With some cleaning methods it may be possible to remove a degree of soiling from parts of the facade which are heavily soiled, thus returning the whole facade to nearer maximum aesthetic value.

After construction, a building might be said to have a certain initial aesthetic value. After a number of years of weathering, where accumulations of soiling are consistent with the architectural features and the stone texture, complexity is increased and aesthetic value rises to a peak. Thereafter, it begins to decline as soiling increases, becoming unrelated to underlying architectural features. As soiling becomes increasingly heavy, complexity is reduced and aesthetic value decreases to a point where the whole facade is blackened and complexity is at a minimum. In Figure 3.1, cleaning a building at the point of maximum soiling has the effect of returning it to an earlier point on the graph, and the soiling cycle is again reintroduced. The point at which it returns and the subsequent soiling effects may well depend on the method chosen for cleaning and the success of the cleaning process.

The relationship between soiling, architecture and aesthetics is complex and is subject to differences between individuals. Figure 3.1 may represent the general position. The main point here is that soiling need not always be aesthetically detrimental and can sometimes be aesthetically beneficial (Plate 3.27). Andrew (1992) gives an account of the relationship between aesthetics, visual complexity and building soiling.

Plate 3.27 Provans Lordship House, Glasgow.
This rubble building has been cleaned. The light level of soiling on its facade adds to the visual complexity and aesthetic appeal of the building.

3.4 Aesthetic considerations checklist

The following list provides a basic checklist for aesthetic considerations to be made before any decisions on cleaning should be taken.

Townscaping

* What is the level of soiling on the building which is being considered for cleaning, in terms of the urban area within which it exists?

* Will cleaning this individual building detract from or enhance the sense of place of the region?

Streetscaping

* Is the building part of a street or other unified facade which should be read as whole and which cleaning would destroy?

* What will be the aesthetic effect of cleaning a single building in terms of nearby buildings?

* If the building is being cleaned as part of a more extensive cleaning programme, what measures are being taken to ensure consistency of finished results between the various buildings?

Architecture

* What are the surface textures of the stones and have these influenced the attachment of soiling?

* Does the level of soiling in any way add to the complexity or visual appeal of the building?

* Has a detailed survey been conducted of stonework of the building to ascertain what defects, such as staining or blemishes, might be more apparent after cleaning?

* To what extent will any highlighted blemishes adversely affect the final appearance of the building?

* What will be the nature and extent of the indenting work required and what will be the initial and long term aesthetic implications?

Cleaning

* What will be aesthetically the most pleasing end result of cleaning in terms of the proportion and location of soiling to be removed? Is partial cleaning a possible option for cleaning?

* What will be the colour of the stone following the various cleaning options and what are the implications in terms of neighbouring buildings?

Chapter 4 Physical cleaning methods

4.1 Physical cleaning

Physical cleaning methods embrace a wide variety of techniques. Although most work on the principle of abrading the surface layer of stone to which soiling is attached, there is considerable variation in the effects which different techniques have on stone. Common physical cleaning methods include water washing and grit blasting. The roughening and erosion of the stone surface which may take place is particularly important when considering the use of any physical cleaning method. The amount of erosion and roughening that occurs is dependent on a range of factors. These include the type and physical state of the stone, the pressure used and the nature and size of any abrading particles used in the cleaning process. Also of vital importance is the skill and training of the operative employed on the cleaning task. Commercial pressures to clean buildings quickly can lead to the abuse of many physical cleaning methods with resulting damage to stonework.

With physical cleaning methods any problems or damage which may arise as a result of cleaning are usually apparent at the time of cleaning, although surface roughening and erosion may not always be obvious to the untrained eye. In recent years there has been a proliferation of new physical cleaning techniques which claim to have little damaging effect on stone. Many of these techniques, while promising, have yet to undergo the extensive scientific testing necessary to evaluate their performance.

4.2 Water washing

Low pressure water washing

A distinction can to be made between water washing at low (mains) and high pressure. Low pressure water washing is probably the least aggressive method of stonecleaning. It is commonly used to clean limestone where dirt is generally bound to relatively soluble chemical compounds. It is also used to clean marble, polished granite and some bricks, where water soluble particles are readily removed by the application of water and brushing. More stubborn soiling can be softened with water and then mechanically removed by non-ferrous brushes (to avoid iron staining). Low pressure water washing can be used on sandstones where loosely attached particles can be removed. In situations where only this level of cleaning is required, low pressure water washing can be effective. Water washing does not remove more stubborn soiling on sandstones where the soiling is bound to the silicate surface in insoluble compounds.

Water washing involves using the minimum amount of water sufficient to wash the deposits away, or loosening them enough to allow them to be mechanically removed. Cleaning should begin from the top of the building to avoid washing dirt onto previously cleaned surfaces. The time taken to clean varies significantly depending on the nature of the surface to be cleaned. Smooth flat surfaces may be cleaned relatively quickly, while intricate stonework with heavy soiling may take much longer.

Intermittent (or pulse) washing is a newer technique where spray times are controlled electronically, or by using clocks, to reduce the amount of water saturation of the stone. Spray times of a few seconds are followed by a few minutes shut-down. This allows softening of the dirt while minimising the problem of saturation (Ashurst, 1988).

Water washing and brushing is also used as a preliminary to chemical cleaning. Loose or water soluble material removed by water washing reduces the amount of chemicals needed.

Water washing at low pressures can be effective at removing some organic growths (e.g. algae).

In some situations (e.g. cleaning limestones) fine or nebulous sprays of clean, cold water are misted over the surface of the stone. Mains water is normally used. With limestones, hard water should be used since water containing dissolved carbon dioxide (CO_2) is acidic and can corrode the stone (Amoroso and Fassina, 1983).

High pressure water washing

High pressure water washing is conducted at a range of pressures, up to 13,800 kPa (2000 psi) or more. Water at higher pressures is always more abrasive than at the lower pressures, although with some more durable stone types there may be no visible erosive effect even at very high pressures. Sandstones vary widely in their hardness and softer varieties may be severely eroded even at relatively low pressures.

Water at higher pressure has a cutting action, and both the design of the outlet lance and the skill of the operative are important in terms of cleaning effects. The spread of the nozzle in particular is important as it influences the pressure of the water at the surface of the stone. Straight ahead nozzles with 0 to 15 degrees of spread are to be avoided on vulnerable stone since the concentrated energy can be damaging. For architectural cleaning, nozzles with 15 to 50 degree spreads are commonly used. The distance that the nozzle is held from the surface and its angle also influences the actual water pressure on the stone. It should be remembered that the water pressure indicated on machinery dials used in cleaning is not necessarily the same as the pressure of water at the stone face. The pressure used should be chosen so as not to damage the stone. At pressures as low as 1,380 kPa (200 psi) water may have an abrasive action on soft stones. On soft stone, or on damaged areas, the use of high pressures can be devastating. Black (1977) notes that in one example pressures of 4,140 kPa (600 psi) were effective at removing soot deposits from sandstone but caused erosion in apparently sound sandstone and disaggregation of friable areas.

Another important consideration is the volume of water used. This may range from 4.5 l/min. (1 gallon/min.) for delicate work up to 36 l/min. (8 gallons/min.). When cleaning sandstone it is normal for the water to be heated to improve the cleaning action.

High pressure water washing can be very effective at removing organic growth, although it will generally not remove soiling from severely soiled sandstone. The possible damage to stonework from high pressure water should always be considered before any use of this method.

The water lance is also used for rinsing after wet grit blasting or chemical cleaning where it washes off dirt or chemicals remaining on the stone surface (see Chapter 5).

Technical problems associated with water washing

The technical problems associated with low pressure water washing also apply to high pressure water washing. The potentially destructive effects of high pressure water on stone should not be underestimated, units are available which are capable of doing considerable damage to stone.

Most of the problems associated with long duration water washing methods have to do with saturation of the stone (Ashurst, 1988). Saturation, as a result of water washing, can have a number of adverse effects. Deep penetration of water into the stone may drive dirt or salts deep into the interior which are then difficult to remove. If salts mobilised by the cleaning water migrate to the surface of the stone this can cause efflorescences and discolouration.

Ashurst (1988) suggests that washing can result in brown staining appearing on the surface of some types of stone (most noticeable on light coloured stones) caused by tarry residues washing out of the pores or as water dries out from the stones and joints. This may be a problem where soiling is particularly heavy and hence is more likely to occur on older buildings.

Decayed or loosened pointing may be lost due to water washing, especially washing at high pressures. Water penetrating through cracks and defective pointing can cause damage if it comes into contact with timbers, iron fixings, electrical wiring and internal fixtures and fittings. Water can also collect in voids within the walls and elsewhere which may lead to direct damage or future problems with rot.

In cold conditions trapped water can freeze resulting in considerable damage to the stone and joints. Ideally, no water washing should take place while there is any danger of this occurring.

Good cleaning practice

The testing procedures recommended in Chapter 6 should be carried out prior to cleaning.

Many problems associated with water washing as a cleaning technique can be avoided by adhering to the rule of applying the minimum amount of water, for the minimum amount of time to the precise place needed. This ideal scenario can be approached by adopting a number of good practice measures.

Care should be taken to use the lowest pressure which achieves the desired level of cleaning. Special care should be taken on areas of decayed or damaged stone. Even at the lowest pressure, any loose or spalling material is likely to be lost. The water pressure at the stone surface is not only affected by the pressure set on the machine but also by the distance of the nozzle from the stone and its angle. Impact pressure decreases rapidly with increasing distance from the stone surface and with increasing angle of incidence.

Brushing the facade should commence as soon as the surface deposits become soft enough to be dislodged.

The problem of excess run-off water down the building face can be reduced by the use of splash boards and sheeting. These are attached at intervals to the facade and channel the water away via downpipes.

The question of whether to re-point before or after high pressure water washing sometime arises. As cleaning by this method can damage jointing material, it is usual to repoint after cleaning. However, in situations where the original jointing material is either absent or in a condition which would allow excessive amounts of water to ingress into the building, it may be advantageous to re-point before cleaning. If any mortar is lost in the cleaning process repointing will be necessary.

Water washing at high pressure is often used to remove chemicals from the stone surface or to wash off the residues of wet grit blasting. Research (Webster *et al.*, 1992) suggests that high pressure water washing is generally little more effective than washing at lower pressures. Using lower pressures also reduces the potential damage which may be caused to the stone by using higher pressure methods.

In the cleaning of limestones, the use of systems which employ a continuous wet mist over the building reduces the total quantity of water applied to the facade. In practice the effectiveness of mist systems depends on how effectively the mist can be contained, as even with tightly sheeted scaffolding draughts of air carry the water mist away from the building (Ashurst, 1988).

Steam cleaning

Steam cleaning, commonly used in the inter-war period, is infrequently used today. When used in conjunction with mild detergents it can remove grease and oil. It is also useful in situations where other methods are difficult to use (e.g. on irregular surfaces) where it loosens dirt by causing it to swell and become detached. Steam cleaning should be followed by scrubbing as in the case of water washing. It is effective at removing organic growth but is slow, expensive and potentially dangerous for the operative. It is considered by some authors to be little better than cold water washing (Ashurst, 1972, 1975, 1988) and is ineffective at removing severe staining.

4.3 Grit blasting techniques

Grit blasting covers a wide range of techniques. Most methods fall into one of two broad categories; dry grit blasting and wet grit blasting. In recent years grit blasting techniques have become increasingly more sophisticated. Equipment is becoming available which is more controllable in terms of pressures used and methods of operation. The range and type of grit blasting particles, as well as the methods available for delivery have increased enormously. Many of these new techniques have been designed to be less damaging to the stonework than existing methods. However, most have not yet been subjected to independent scientific investigation.

Dry grit blasting

In dry grit blasting the abrasive material is blown against the surface by a stream of compressed air to scour away the soiling. In its simplest form the equipment required consists of an air compressor, abrasive and air delivery pipes and a container for the abrasive material. Dry grit blasting can remove heavy soiling from stone (Plates 4.1 and 4.2). Ideally, only the soiled surface layer should be removed but in practice this is difficult to control and it is easy to cause damage to a building using this method of cleaning (Plate 4.3 and 4.4).

Abrasives used in the past were often sand or flint containing free silica which exposed operatives and the public to the danger of lung damage. Abrasives containing free silica are no longer permitted. Abrasives used today include mineral slags, olivine and aluminium oxide. Even such materials as corn husks, egg shells, glass beads and walnut shells have been employed as abrasives. The abrasive used must be free of iron oxide as any residue left in the stone could cause staining.

Various sizes of nozzle are available to deliver the abrasive to the stone. These need to be carefully selected. Ashurst (1988) suggests long venturi nozzles are effective on flat areas with even soiling as they deliver particles evenly over a wide area. With detailed stonework a thinner pencil shaped blast is required. Ideally, nozzles should deliver a constant flow of abrasive to the stonework with the air/grit mix at any pressure set as lean as possible (Ashurst, 1988).

The size of grit particles used can be altered to suit the conditions. Fine grits are usually used for delicate work, carvings and friable surfaces. Coarser grits may be employed in other situations. The type of abrasive used is in part determined by stone and soiling type. In the past, spherical abrasives such as glass bead have been used to remove compacted soiling on hard rocks such as granite. Angular abrasives, such as blasting grits have a cutting action and are more suited to softer soiling (Ashurst, 1988). The absence of the use of water means there is no risk of staining, efflorescences or frost damage.

Pressures used for dry grit blasting typically range from as low as 50 kPa up to 700 kPa (7psi to 100psi). Damage can occur at any pressure but is more likely at higher pressures. Dry grit blasting techniques are easily misused. Operatives may increase the pressure of blasting to speed up the cleaning process.

With sandstones, dry grit blasting works by removing the layer of stone to which the soiling is attached. Young and Urquhart (1992) conducted microscopic examinations of sandstones cleaned by dry grit blasting at 550 kPa (80 psi). Results showed that in the samples studied, little or no shattering of surface grains occurred, indicating that cleaning occurs in association with grain loss rather than by shattering of the surface. If this method is to be effective in removing the soiling, then the sandstone surface will have to be eroded back until the thickness of the soiled layer is removed. This soiled layer usually penetrates to no more than about 1 or 2 grain thickness deep. The thickness of the soiling layer itself is usually no more than a few μm thick (e.g. 10-100 μm). The actual depth of soiling penetration depends to a large extent on the grain size of the sandstone as well as its porosity and degree of soiling (Fig 4.1).

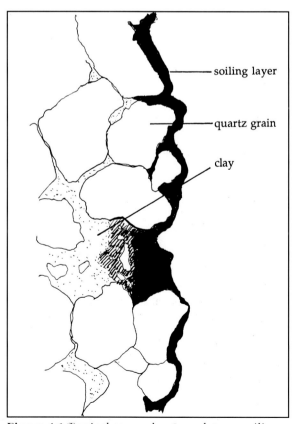

Figure 4.1 Typical example of sandstone soiling.

soiling layer

quartz grain

clay

Plate 4.1 Sandstone building before grit blasting. Note how soiling on smooth faced stones tends to follow particular horizons.

Plate 4.2 After cleaning (same area as above). Most soiling has been removed. Some ingrained soiling remains.

Plate 4.3 Damage to a sandstone building caused by dry grit blasting.

Plate 4.4 Damage to detailing caused by dry grit blasting.

51

Technical problems associated with dry grit blasting

Most of the problems associated with dry grit blasting involve erosion and surface roughening. Research into sandstone cleaning by Young and Urquhart (1992) shows that it is usually the case that higher abrasive pressures produce greater degrees of erosion. The higher the grit blasting pressure the more critical is the physical nature of the stone in controlling the amount of abrasion. As dry grit blasting works by the erosion of the surface layer, stone with ingrained soiling should not be cleaned by this method, unless the intention is to leave the more ingrained soiling in place.

Sandstone types which contain calcite cemented areas can be affected by pitting of the surface following cleaning (Plate 4.5). Pitting develops if sandstones contain irregularly distributed calcite cements. As calcite cements are much weaker than most other cements, the calcite cemented patches are more rapidly eroded by abrasive cleaning. Removal of the calcite inevitably leads to the loss of the sand grains if they are held together only by the cement. The end result is pitting of the surface of the sandstone.

Where there is a difference in hardness between the layers of a sedimentary stone, grit blasting can erode away the softer material and exaggerate the stone's bedding planes (Plate 4.6). Whilst cleaning, areas of stonework may be encountered which are very easily eroded and which might not have been present on trial test panels.

Surface roughening occurs in many stones subjected to dry grit blasting. Smooth surfaced sandstones are almost invariably roughened following cleaning and on detailed surfaces, sharpness of outline may be lost. A rough surface can increase the susceptibility of a stone to water retention, further pollution and dirt deposition. Stone which is damaged, spalling or badly decayed is likely to be severely affected by grit blasting (Plates 4.7 and 4.8).

Research by Young and Urquhart (1992) using scanning electron microscope (SEM) examination of the surface of freshly cut sandstones following dry grit blast cleaning, showed the presence of large amounts of surface debris and, where clays were present, these were often pulverised where they had been exposed to abrasion (Plate 4.9 and 4.10). Both surface debris and broken clays may clog the surface pores and reduce the permeability of the surface of abrasively cleaned sandstones.

Plate 4.5 Pitting of sandstone following dry grit blasting, due to erosion of calcite cemented areas.

Plate 4.6 The relief of this stone's bedding planes has been exaggerated by cleaning which preferentially eroded the softer layers.

Plate 4.7 Decayed sandstone with spalling, soiled surfaces before cleaning.

Plate 4.8 After cleaning (same area as above). Spalling surfaces completely removed by cleaning.

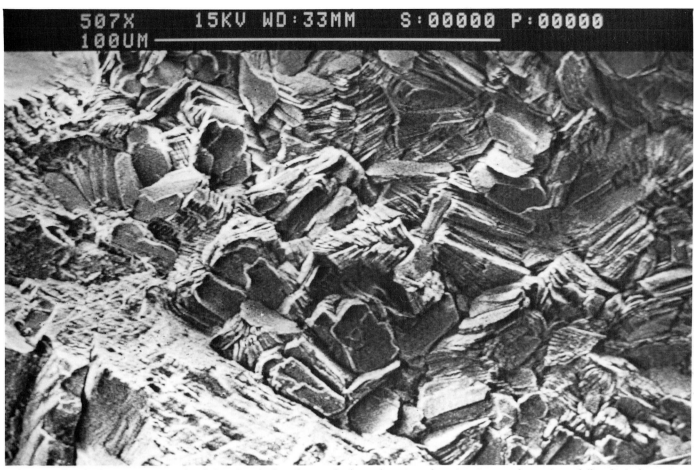

Plate 4.9 SEM photomicrograph of Cat Castle Sandstone before cleaning showing intact clay mineral (kaolinite).

Plate 4.10 SEM photomicrograph of Cat Castle Sandstone after cleaning by dry grit blasting at 80psi. The clay minerals to the left (kaolinite) have been pulverised by impact and there is a lot of debris on the stone surface.

Good cleaning practice

Testing procedures as recommended in Chapter 6 should be carried out prior to cleaning.

It is essential when contemplating dry grit blasting to understand the physical characteristics of the stone, and to note the presence of any decayed or spalling stone, since this will almost certainly be eroded by cleaning. Dry grit blasting should not be used on polished surfaces or on areas of delicate architectural detail or carvings.

The pressure used in dry grit blasting should be the minimum necessary to produce a level of cleaning consistent with the least damage to the stone. The hardness and size of the abrasives used needs to be considered against the softness of the stone. It might be the case that a range of different abrasive particle sizes are used on a particular building depending on conditions.

Dry grit blasting should be followed by low pressure water washing if any surface debris remains on the stone. This debris is unsightly and if left on the stone, may speed the resoiling process.

The residues from dry (and wet) grit blasting can block gutters, downpipes and even sewers. Care should be taken to avoid this problem.

Dry grit blasting produces considerable amounts of dust. This can ingress into buildings through the smallest opening. All necessary precautions should be taken to ensure this is avoided. The nuisance from dust can, to a large extent, be reduced by screening the scaffolding with sheeting and sealing off windows and other places where dust can ingress.

Abrasive cleaning can be very hazardous to operatives and those in the vicinity of the cleaning operation. Lung damage can be caused by inhaling airborne silica, dust and debris from cleaning. Even when a non-silica abrasive is used, silica can be released from the stone surface. Sandstones, granites and some limestones contain silica in the form of quartz and if the surface is abraded, this silica will be released into the atmosphere. Operatives must wear proper protective clothing, including "air-line" helmets which supply a constant stream of clean air inside the helmet.

Noise, particularly from the delivery nozzle and the impact of the air and abrasive mix on the stonework can be problematic and is difficult to avoid. Forewarning those likely to be affected by noise can at least be done. Compressors should be sited so as to reduce, as far as possible, noise from this source.

As dry grit blasting is a method which can cause considerable damage in the hands of unskilled operatives, training and proper supervision is essential.

Wet grit blasting

This method is similar to dry grit blasting except that water is introduced into the air/grit stream to make a slurry, which is then delivered to the stone with either a single large or several small jets. The process uses a minimum amount of water and produces much less dust than dry grit blasting.

Wet grit blasting can be very effective at removing heavy soiling which is not ingrained into the stone (Plates 4.11 and 4.12).

Technological advances have been made with wet grit blasting. Equipment is becoming available which delivers the air, water and abrasive in a range of different possible permutations. Some newer wet grit blasting systems operate with lower pressures and smaller amounts of grit than in the past. A range of alternative abrasive materials are also being tried out. Sodium bicarbonate for instance, is sometimes used as an alternative to harder abrasive particles. Many of these systems await independent scientific testing.

Technical problems associated with wet grit blasting

Many of the difficulties associated with dry grit blasting are also common to wet grit blasting, particularly those associated with surface roughening and erosion. Pressure of the water/grit mix at the stone surface is the most critical factor governing surface roughening and erosion of the stone. Young and Urquhart (1992) found little difference between dry and wet grit blasting at similar pressures in terms of surface erosion and roughening. Operator control is also critical and, apart from blasting pressure, is probably one of the main factors influencing the amount of erosion and surface roughening that occurs.

Wet grit blasting is ineffective at removing sub-surface soiling. As water is used, there is a danger of efflorescences due to the mobilisation of salts within the stone. There is also the potential problem of water penetrating the building. Loose or damaged pointing should be replaced prior to cleaning to prevent water ingress. If any mortar is lost in the cleaning process repointing will be necessary. Wet grit blasting should be halted where there is any possibility that water entering the stone could freeze.

Clouds of wet spray can hamper the vision of operatives resulting in an uneven clean (gun-shading). This is caused by differential erosion as a result of uneven application across the surface. Problems can often arise with clogging of equipment. As a result, operatives are sometimes tempted to turn off the water supply, in effect reverting to dry grit blasting.

Plate 4.11 Heavily soiled sandstone prior to wet blast cleaning. There is severe soiling on the exposed ledge and typical soiling of smooth, vertical stonework under the ledge.

Plate 4.12 After cleaning (same area as above). Following cleaning virtually all soiling has been removed, but there is a thick crusting of loose dust and debris from wet grit blasting coating the surface.

Good cleaning practice

Testing procedures as recommended in Chapter 6 should be carried out prior to cleaning.

It is essential when contemplating wet grit blasting to understand the physical characteristics of the stone, and to note the presence of any decayed or spalling stone, since this will almost certainly be eroded by wet grit blasting. Wet grit blasting should not be used on polished surfaces or on areas of delicate architectural detail or carvings.

The pressure used in wet grit blasting should be the minimum necessary to produce a level of cleaning consistent with the least damage to the stone. The hardness and size of the abrasives used needs to be considered. It might be the case that a range of different abrasive particle sizes and pressures are used on a particular building depending on conditions.

It is essential following wet grit blasting, that the masonry is properly washed down. High pressure, low volume water lances have been commonly used for this task, although low pressure washing is, in most cases, just as effective and avoids the risks inherent in using high pressure. Failure to thoroughly wash down masonry after wet grit blasting results in dust and debris adhering as a hard crust to the surface of the stone (Plates 4.13 and 4.14). Care must be taken to ensure that sludge is removed from all places where it can collect such as on or under ledges and behind downpipes. This washing should commence from the top of the building to avoid washing debris onto previously cleaned areas. Any build up of sludge on the ground or under scaffolding should be regularly removed to prevent blockage of drains. Care should also be taken to ensure that debris does not wash over and dry on adjacent facades (Plate 4.15).

Plate 4.13 Dust and debris coating the sandstone surface after wet grit blasting.

Plate 4.14 Hardened rock dust/grit deposited on this stonework as a result of wet grit blasting is disfiguring the architectural detailing.

Plate 4.15 Debris wash over on to the next facade after wet grit blasting.

Low pressure dry grit blasting

Low pressure grit blasting was originally developed as a tool in museum conservation work for restoration and cleaning of delicate objects. In recent years the technique has been scaled up for use in stonecleaning. The method involves combining finely graded abrasive powder (for example aluminium oxide) with compressed air at very low pressure. This is directed onto the stone using a small nozzled gun (Plate 4.16). Pressures used are commonly in the range 20 kPa to 35 kPa (3 to 5 psi).

This method of cleaning is claimed to have advantages over other physical methods of cleaning. In some cleaning situations it has a minimal effect on the physical structure of the stone (Plate 4.17). Under ideal circumstances the method can be effective at removing heavy surface soiling whilst retaining the natural patina of the stone. Erosion of the stone often appears to be negligible and delicate tooling marks may be retained (Plates 4.18 and 4.19). With some types of stone this method is not always effective at removing soiling (Plate 4.20).

Plate 4.16 Low pressure grit blasting in operation.

Plate 4.17 Sandstone partially cleaned using low pressure grit blasting. No apparent erosion along edge of the stone.

Plate 4.18 Sandstone partially cleaned using low pressure grit blasting. Right side of corner cleaned, left side uncleaned. The left side shows soiling at the top and a naturally unsoiled area to lower left. The cleaned area to the right was originally black with soiling. Its appearance now resembles the natural weathered patina. Tool marks are retained.

Plate 4.19 Sandstone partially cleaned using low pressure grit blasting. Most soiling has been removed and tool marks are retained.

Plate 4.20 Test panel cleaned using low pressure grit blasting. Surface soiling has largely been removed, more ingrained soiling remains.

Technical problems associated with low pressure dry grit blasting

Low pressure blasting is not always effective in removing more ingrained soiling and thickly encrusted organic growth (Plate 4.21). Buildings cleaned using this method may well retain appreciable amounts of visible soiling (Plate 4.22). Ideally the method should remove soiling from between stone grains without eroding the grains themselves. If the gaps between grains are much smaller than the grade of grit used, cleaning may be unsuccessful (Fig 4.2) (Urquhart *et al.*, 1992).

The method does allow for a high degree of operative control and the cleaning can be quickly stopped if any difficulties are encountered. On some stone types erosion and surface roughening can occur. As low pressures are used, the problem of airborne dust and debris is reduced.

Good cleaning practice

Testing procedures as recommended in Chapter 6 should be carried out prior to cleaning.

The points raised in connection with dry grit blasting also apply to low pressure grit blasting.

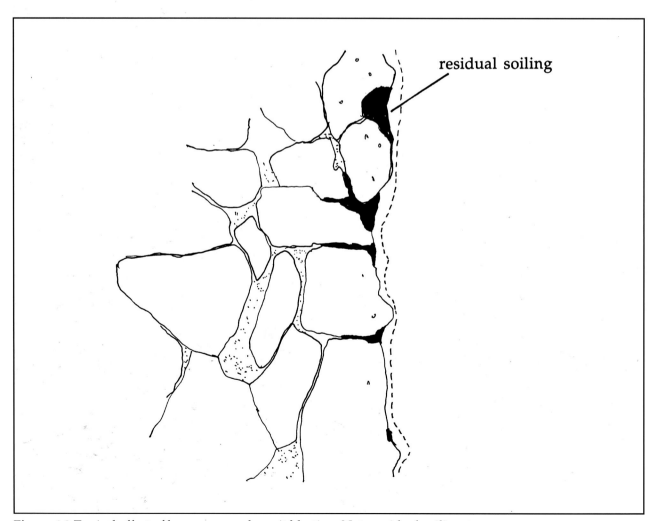

Figure 4.2 Typical effect of low pressure dry grit blasting. Note residual soiling.

Plate 4.21 This thickly encrusted organic growth has not been removed by low pressure grit blasting.

Plate 4.22 Sandstone building cleaned by low pressure grit blasting. Some soiling is still visible on the facade.

4.4 Mechanical cleaning

A variety of techniques, including the use of brushes, discs, abrasive block and needle guns can be grouped under the general heading of mechanical cleaning methods. These work by abrading and removing the surface of the stone, removing the surface layer and thereby exposing fresh stone. The use of some of these methods can be particularly damaging since they remove the surface patina and blur tooled detailing on the stone surface. In the past, considerable damage has been caused by these methods. While virtually never used today as the principal method of cleaning a building, they are occasionally used to remove stubborn stains which remain following other cleaning treatments.

Disc cleaning

Disc cleaning involves the use of carborundum discs and brushes attached to power tools and applied directly to the surface of the stone. A range of different discs and brushes are available to suit the work being undertaken. Undoubtedly this is the most damaging form of mechanical cleaning, particularly as the considerable abrasive power of the machines is very difficult to control, even in the most skilled hands. Typical forms of damage include the distortion of straight arrises and loss of original surfacing on flat surfaces and carved details. Mechanical grinding can result in the scouring of facade surfaces and the "imprinting" of the disc as a series of curved, shallow hollows on the stone surface. Disc cleaning results in the re-dressing of the stone.

Dry brushing

This involves manually brushing the facade with a stiff bristle or nylon brushing to remove organic growth and loosely bound surface dirt. Sometimes a commercial grade vacuum cleaner is used to take away the debris as it is removed from the surface. More ingrained soiling will not be removed by this method. It can be effective on rubble and rock faced ashlar buildings where soiling is less noticeable or where only a low level of cleaning is required (Plate 4.23).

Plate 4.23 A rubble constructed building cleaned by dry brushing.

4.5 Effects of abrasive cleaning on sandstone facades

Most abrasive cleaning methods work by removing a layer of grains from the surface of the facade and with it the outer soiled layer. It is unlikely that the colour of stone exposed below the soiling will be identical to that of the fresh stone.

On facades of smooth stone a minimum of surface area is exposed to abrasion. Tooled surfaces expose a slightly greater area and may therefore experience somewhat greater degrees of abrasion. The greatest surface areas of stone will be exposed at corners of blocks and in areas of detail. Here the potential for material loss will be much greater. Note that such exposed areas of stone may also be suffering from the worst effects of decay and deterioration. This loss of material can lead to loss of detail, rounding of sharp edges and the distortion of arrises (Plate 4.24). Areas of spalling or decayed stone will not survive most abrasive cleaning.

Roughening can be caused simply by the removal of a layer of grains from the sandstone surface. In coarser grained sandstones this will lead to a greater degree of roughening than in finer grained sandstones.

Grit blasting generally erodes the surface of the sandstone unevenly. Variability introduced by the operator and variations in the physical characteristics of the sandstone make it almost impossible to clean a sandstone facade using abrasives without causing some roughening. The amount of roughening which can be caused is greater at higher grit blasting pressures.

A compact, well cemented sandstone may be only minimally affected even by high pressure abrasive cleaning. A less dense, lightly compacted sandstone with less cementing material is more vulnerable to abrasion and may be seriously eroded even at relatively low grit blasting pressures.

Uneven surface erosion can result where there are differences in the hardness of the minerals which make up the sandstone. This applies both to mineral grains and cements. Calcareous sandstones are especially vulnerable to this type of surface roughening since calcite cemented areas are more easily eroded than the surrounding sandstone. Variable loss of material from particular bedding layers, resulting from differences in mineralogy or grain size, will result in different degrees of erosion on individual stone blocks. Sandstones in building facades are normally placed with their natural bedding planes horizontal. If cleaning results in raised ridges across the sandstone surface these will trap soiling washed down the facade by rainwater resulting in increased rates of resoiling and increased levels of water uptake.

Most physical cleaning methods are effective in removing superficial algal growth from sandstone (Plates 4.25 and 4.26), although the potential damage to stone should always be considered before they are used.

The method adopted to clean sandstone should be selected so as to produce a level of cleaning consistent with the least damage to the stone.

Plate 4.24 Following cleaning this arris is no longer straight, as the shadow shows.

Plate 4.25 Before wet grit blast cleaning. Algal growth below window ledge.

Plate 4.26 After wet grit blast cleaning (same area as above). Algal growth completely removed.

4.6 Resoiling of facades following abrasive cleaning

It is likely that a stone surface roughened by abrasive cleaning will resoil at an accelerated rate compared with a smooth surface, since a rough surface is more efficient at trapping particulate soiling and water.

Following cleaning, a rougher surface with, as a consequence, a greater degree of exposed surface area, may be more hospitable to biological organisms. Water run-off rates will be slower over a rougher surface. Slower run-off may increase the depth of penetration of absorbed water where such run-off is concentrated. Such areas may, therefore, remain damp for longer periods following wetting, encouraging organic growths and attracting more soiling.

The surface debris which results from abrasive cleaning, if not fully removed, can be washed into pores on the surface of the sandstone, and may affect water absorption and evaporation rates which can potentially affect the resoiling rate of a facade. The debris in itself will trap both organic and inorganic soiling.

The rate of resoiling will also be dependent on the location of the building, its orientation and on local atmospheric conditions.

4.7 Summary of the effects of physical cleaning

A number of general conclusions can be drawn with regard to the various physical methods of cleaning stone.

Water washing consists of applying water, with or without hand brushing, at either low or high pressure to the building facade to remove the soiling. Water washing is a commonly used method to clean limestone but is much less effective at removing the more strongly bound soiling from sandstones and granites. Apart from the problem of water saturation, low pressure water washing is relatively problem free. High pressure water washing can be physically damaging to stone, particularly soft sedimentary or decaying stone.

Dry and wet grit blasting are two common methods of abrasive cleaning. Both methods can be effective at removing soiling, but carry a number of consequences. The two significant forms of damage due to abrasive cleaning are erosion and surface roughening. The degree of erosion and surface roughening depend mainly on the blast pressure adopted and the dwell-time of the jet on the stone surface. The blast pressure at the stone surface is not only affected by the pressure set on the machine but also by the distance of the nozzle from the stone. Pressure decreases rapidly with increasing distance from the stone surface. As might be expected, coarser grained stones have been found to suffer a greater degree of surface erosion than fine grained stones, due to the removal of the larger grain particles. Complete removal of soiling from a stone can only be effected by eroding the surface of the stone back until the thickness of the soiled layer is removed. The soiled layer on a sandstone normally extends to a depth of one or two grain diameters.

The amount of erosion suffered is related to the exposed surface area of the stone. A smooth dressed stone exposes a minimum area, whereas a stone with a tooled or detailed surface will expose a significantly increased surface area and will consequently suffer increased erosion. The use of abrasive cleaning techniques on a tooled surface can have very variable results, depending on the nature of the abrasive cleaning used.

Abrasive methods can change the original surface texture of sandstones which have a pronounced fabric. The loss of material will tend to be greater on the softer, less resistant layers.

No salts or other chemicals are introduced into the stone, so the only occasion when efflorescence might result would be following wet cleaning if salts were previously present in the stone.

Low pressure grit blasting is designed to reduce the type of damage caused by high pressure blast methods. It can be effective at removing superficial soiling from stone, although it may not remove more ingrained soiling. Erosion and roughening may still occur on vulnerable stones.

Mechanical cleaning methods embrace a number of techniques from dry brushing by hand to discs and brushes used in conjunction with power tools. This form of cleaning is rarely used in isolation from other forms of cleaning. Cleaning devices attached to power tools are capable of doing considerable damage to stone, even in experienced hands.

With physical cleaning in general, operator control in conjunction with the pressure used, is the critical factor influencing the amount of stone erosion and surface roughening which may occur. On-site quality control and effective operator training are therefore the key elements in reducing the degree of damage to the stone when using physical cleaning techniques.

Unlike chemical cleaning methods, the cleaning can be stopped quickly if problems arise. Although often not removing all soiling from stone, quite pleasing results can sometimes be achieved especially with the less aggressive methods.

Aesthetically pleasing results may be achieved without complete removal of soiling. With all abrasive methods of cleaning the method selected should be consistent with the least damage to the stone.

Chapter 5   Chemical cleaning methods

5.1 Chemical cleaning regimes

Chemical cleaning methods work by chemical reaction between the cleaning agent, soiling and the masonry surface to which the soiling is attached. A wide range of chemical cleaning agents is available commercially, but all can be categorised into a few groups according to their chemical and physical properties. Methods recommended for their use also vary between manufacturers. A liquid acid cleaning regime might involve the following steps:-

1.   Pre-wet the stone.
2.   Apply alkaline degreaser and allow to dwell for an appropriate length of time.
3.   Thoroughly wash off with high pressure water spray.
4.   Apply acid cleaner and allow to dwell for the correct length of time.
5.   Wash off with high pressure water spray.

An alkaline poultice cleaning programme might involve:-

1.   Application of poultice to dry stone.
2.   Cover with plastic sheet to prevent drying.
3.   Leave for stated time.
4.   Unwrap and scrape off poultice.
5.   Rinse off with water.
6.   Apply neutralising wash and allow to dwell for stated time.
7.   Wash with high pressure water spray.

Chemical cleaning agents

Chemical cleaners range from acids through to alkalis. The active ingredient may be a single component material or a mixture and can vary considerably in concentration as well as strength. Table 5.1 shows some common active components.

The physical nature of cleaning agents is usually modified by the addition of relatively inert materials which control the viscosity. Thus the acids and alkalis which are the active ingredients may be presented as fairly mobile liquids, thixotropes, gels or pastes (poultices). Other additives may include detergents and biocides. Technical literature from the manufacturers, suitable for contractors, is usually supplied with the cleaning agent. However modification of chemical strengths or dwell times may be necessary if indicated by analysis of test panel results. In commercial practice, procedures are often adapted to suit particular situations. It should be stressed that where procedures are adapted, this should be done on the basis of scientific analysis of test panel cleaning (see Chapter 6), and not simply on a visual inspection of the cleaned stone.

Table 5.1 Common active components of chemical cleaning agents.

Active Ingredients		
Alkalis : Sodium hydroxide Ammonia Sodium carbonate Sodium bicarbonate	Decreasing base strength	
Acids : Hydrochloric acid Sulphuric acid Phosphoric acid Hydrofluoric acid Ammonium hydrogen fluoride	Decreasing acid strength	

5.2 Chemical cleaning of sandstones

The action of chemical cleaning agents on sandstone

Research by Webster *et al.* (1992) on the cleaning of sandstones points to a number of effects of chemical cleaning agents. Hydrofluoric acid (HF) based chemical cleaners appear to work by dissolving the surface layer of sandstone (normally only a few microns in thickness) to which the soiling is attached. The soiling is then removed, along with some dissolved and loosened sandstone, when the facade is washed down. The amount of sandstone which is dissolved in this process is small compared to the amount of material which is abraded by many physical cleaning methods. However, some solid material can be lost if the chemical treatment attacks and loosens cementing minerals in the sandstone. Grains can be lost from the sandstone surface where the cementing matrix has been removed. Grain loss may be particularly marked where the cementing matrix is highly soluble in the cleaning chemicals.

Some sandstones contain calcite ($CaCO_3$) as a cementing mineral. The calcite may be distributed throughout the body of the sandstone, but if the calcite is concentrated within particular areas of the sandstone, preferential erosion by acidic chemical cleaning agents may result in surface pitting (Plate 5.1).

Research by Webster *et al.* (1992), adopting standardised laboratory test procedures on freshly cut sandstone, has shown that any given sandstone can behave quite differently under different acid cleaning regimes. These results may not reflect what occurs in commercial practice, where cleaning regimes are varied to suit different stone types, but this research demonstrates the potential of chemical cleaning regimes to damage stone by direct action.

Plate 5.1 Pitting of a sandstone surface caused by removal of calcite by acid cleaning.

Penetration and retention of chemicals in sandstone

Sandstones are often highly porous and permeable. Whenever chemicals are applied to sandstone, no matter how carefully the sandstone is washed down afterwards, some chemicals will inevitably be left behind in the stone. Chemicals may gain access to the interior of the sandstone either through surface penetration or through joints where pointing has deteriorated. Chemicals remaining in sandstone after cleaning have the potential to create a number of problems. These may be apparent visually but can also be insidious, as subtle changes within the stone giving rise to longer term deleterious effects. The danger of chemicals penetrating deeply into stonework via joints can be reduced by replacement of defective pointing before cleaning (see Section 5.6 Mortar repairs).

The changes brought about by absorbed chemicals are very varied and depend on the mineralogical composition of the stone, the pollutants present and the nature of the chemical cleaners themselves. Effects may include the mobilisation of salts and previously stable minerals. Visual consequences may include changes to the stone colour such as bleaching or staining (Plate 5.2), or the precipitation of efflorescences on external surfaces (Plate 5.3). One of the more insidious effects of internal chemical changes is to create pressures within the pores of the stone due to expansion and contraction of salts which hydrate and dehydrate as ambient conditions vary. These hydration pressures can cause accelerated decay.

When these indirect effects, due to the absorption of chemicals, are added to the direct effect of the chemicals dissolving away cementing minerals, the consequences can be very severe in that architectural features can be affected. For instance, surface texture can be altered, architectural quality lost and arrises lose their sharpness.

Research by Webster *et al.* (1992) has shown, by standardised tests on freshly cut stones, that some sandstones have a great propensity to absorb cleaning chemicals. There is a tendency for more porous stones to retain a higher proportion of the applied chemicals than less porous stones. The amounts retained varied from about 40% to 80% of the applied substances in these standardised tests.

The amount of chemicals retained depends to some extent on the orientation of the sandstone bedding planes. The vertical face of a horizontally bedded stone absorbs more than that of a vertically bedded stone. Research has shown that extraction of the absorbed chemicals with water is generally only partially successful, indicating that there are mechanisms which immobilise absorbed chemicals. These mechanisms may include the formation of insoluble salts and interactions with clay minerals. Depth profiling techniques (discussed in Chapter 6) can establish the depth to which chemicals penetrate stone. Laboratory research using freshly cut stone, has shown that cleaning chemicals can penetrate to considerable depths (up to 20mm). The greatest concentration of retained chemicals occurs within 2mm of the surface of the stone. The amount of retained chemicals within the stone tends to decrease progressively from high concentrations near the surface, to lower concentrations within the body of the stone (Webster *et al.*, 1992).

Research on soiled stones has shown that absorption of cleaning chemicals can occur, just as in the case of freshly cut stones. However, the subsequent fate of the absorbed chemicals is complicated by the presence of pollutants. Chemical reactions between the cleaning chemicals, stone and soiling may result in the formation of new chemical compounds in the stone. Relatively large amounts of sulphate are often found in aged sandstones. This is thought to arise from atmospheric pollution, particularly in the form of acid rain (dilute H_2SO_4) which reacts with calcium compounds in the mortar or stone, to form sparingly soluble calcium sulphate ($CaSO_4$). The application of cleaning agents may result in the the solublization of this sulphate. As much as 2% by weight of soluble sulphate has been found in the surface layers of soiled stone after cleaning. In other cases the quantity of soluble sulphate released is much lower (Webster *et al.*, 1992). The quantitative result of cleaning is at present unpredictable, therefore it is essential that individual testing procedures are implemented (Chapter 6).

Research has recently been conducted into the penetration of chemical cleaning agents in the soiled sandstone of the Scott Monument in Edinburgh (Dixon, 1993). The research data relates to trials involving the use of an alkaline poultice and acid afterwash. Sodium residues (from the alkaline poultice) were found in the outer 2-20mm of the sandstone. The penetration of sodium depended on the strengths, application time and consistency of the poultice, the level of soiling of the stone and its state of weathering. The level of sulphate in the stone was generally highest in the outer 2mm before cleaning and was washed further into the stone by cleaning chemicals. Its distribution after cleaning was somewhat irregular. The mechanism of its movement is not fully understood. Depth profiles (Chapter 6) of these and other soluble ions change over time due to natural weathering. Movement of soluble salts where an entire facade has been chemically cleaned is likely to lead to depletion in some areas and concentration (possibly with efflorescence at the surface) in others.

Plate 5.2 Staining caused by the migration of iron from within the stone to the stone surface.

5.3 Efflorescences

One of the most noticeable effects of using chemical cleaning agents on sandstone buildings is the subsequent appearance of efflorescences on the stone surface (Plate 5.3). Efflorescences are soluble salts, usually white, which are mobilised when the stone is wet, then are drawn to the surface of the stone and crystallize as the stone dries out.

Field observations have shown that efflorescences may initially concentrate around joints, where cleaning chemicals are trapped and not washed out, or are washed more deeply into the stone, during the wash-off phase of cleaning. On drying, salts accumulate on surfaces within and around the joint (Plate 5.4). Efflorescences of this nature can be minimised by pointing joints before cleaning.

Efflorescences often form on the same surface areas affected by iron staining and soiling accumulation. These are areas where capillary forces during wetting-drying cycles have concentrated soluble materials at the surface (Plate 5.5). Efflorescences may also concentrate within clay rich layers in sandstone. Efflorescences are ephemeral and come and go as temperature, humidity and moisture levels change in the stone (Plates 5.6 and 5.7).

Efflorescences, apart from their aesthetically detrimental effect, also contribute to decay in sandstones. Two important mechanisms act to cause salt weathering in sandstones, these being hydration pressure and crystallisation pressure. Salt hydration is a process which results in volumetric changes in salts with a resulting pressure increase within the pores of the stone. Some salts (e.g. sodium sulphate) absorb large amounts of water in humid conditions. This results in the dehydrated form of the salt becoming a hydrated form with a greater volume. This expansion can generate very great internal pressures in the stone. Salt crystallisation pressure is similar to the action of frost. It is caused by crystal growth within the pores of the stone. Thus, if as a result of chemical cleaning, residues of salts are left near the surface of a stone, salt decay mechanisms could exacerbate contour scaling and surface decay of the sandstone (Plate 5.8).

Lewin (1982) showed, in a series of experiments using New Hampshire Sandstone, that spalling and blistering can be caused by simple salt crystallisation. Under appropriate conditions, salt (in this case sodium chloride) crystallisation took place within the body of the sandstone. The layer behind which the salt crystallised (approximately 1mm thick) blistered and eventually spalled off, revealing a new surface where the process can begin again (Lewin also recognised the same problem occurring in granite).

In experiments which simulate salt weathering, Goudie (1986) found that salts varied in their ability to break down sandstone. Sodium carbonate (Na_2CO_3) in particular was found to be very destructive in terms of its contribution to sandstone decay. This effect is thought to be due to its high solubility and mobility and the large volume change on hydration. The most destructive salt is sodium sulphate (Na_2SO_4) which has a volume change on hydration of about 300% (Sperling *et al.*, 1985). The nature of the sandstone also has an influence on its susceptibility to salt weathering. Sandstones with a high proportion of microporosity are liable to quite rapid decay from salt hydration pressure.

Frost can also affect salts within sandstone leading to stone decay. Research by Williams and Robinson (1981) showed that, under experimental conditions, freezing and thawing cycles of sandstones containing sodium chloride and sodium sulphate resulted in the almost complete disintegration of some sandstones. Salts cause freezing to take place more slowly, allowing a longer time for larger more damaging crystals to grow in the pore spaces of the stone.

Salt efflorescences can be removed by the use of non ferrous brushes as and when they appear. Attempts to remove them by water washing are likely to result in most of the salts being reabsorbed into the stone only to reappear at a later date.

Plate 5.3 Extensive efflorescences following chemical cleaning.

Plate 5.4 Intense efflorescence of sodium sulphate around an open joint after chemical cleaning.

Plate 5.5 Efflorescences following chemical cleaning occurring in the same places as iron staining and residual soiling. These are areas where capillary forces during wetting/drying cycles have concentrated soluble materials at the surface.

Plate 5.6 Efflorescence shortly after cleaning.

Plate 5.7 Same area as above one month after cleaning, showing temporary disappearance of efflorescences. Efflorescences are ephemeral and come and go as temperature, humidity and moisture levels change in the stone.

Plate 5.8 Efflorescences exacerbate the problem of contour scaling.

5.4 Colour changes following chemical cleaning

Some chemical cleaning agents may dissolve previously stable iron-containing minerals in stone. Through capillary action or moisture evaporating from the surface, this dissolved iron can migrate and be deposited at the stone surface. This iron appears as orange or brown staining on the surface (Plate 5.2). Some manufacturers add phosphoric acid (H_3PO_4) to the cleaning agent to suppress visible migration.

The change in surface colour of the stone following cleaning has been the principal means by which the success or otherwise of the cleaning was judged. Minerals containing iron (Fe) and manganese (Mn), which often occur in very small amounts within the stone, are largely responsible for stone colour.

The variable effect which chemical cleaning can have on stone colour is dramatically illustrated on buildings where individual stones, which cross legal boundaries, have been subjected to different chemical cleaning regimes (Plate 5.9). The dramatic and unsightly changes in stone colour are probably the result of use of chemical cleaners at too high a concentration or of excessive dwell times, or the failure to adapt correctly the cleaning method. The situation is further exacerbated by any time delays between the cleaning of adjacent buildings.

Siliceous minerals (e.g. quartz, feldspar, clay etc.) can, under some conditions, be dissolved and redeposited on the surface of the stone in the form of hard, white, insoluble residues. This is likely to arise from the use of hydrofluoric acid solutions which are too concentrated, or from excessive dwell times. The complexities involved in chemical cleaning emphasise the need for a testing programme and decision making which addresses the various issues and leads to informed specifications for particular situations (Chapter 6).

Plate 5.9 The effect of two different chemical cleaning regimes on a sandstone facade.

5.5 Biological re-growth following cleaning

Following cleaning, buildings may be subject to quite rapid colonisation by algae. There is some evidence (Bluck & Porter, 1991), to suggest that sandstone buildings cleaned by chemical cleaning methods are more susceptible to algal re-growth than those cleaned by abrasive methods. This may be attributable to increased microporosity due to dissolution of quartz and other minerals by hydrofluoric acid and also, in part, be due to retention of cleaning chemicals within the stone. Some constituents of cleaning chemicals, particularly phosphates (present as phosphoric acid (H_3PO_4) in some cleaning fluids) may increase the amount of biological growth by acting as nutrients. Atmospheric pollutants, particularly nitrates may also contribute to biological re-growth.

Chemical cleaning can result in surface roughening of the stone due to dissolution of minerals by stonecleaning chemicals. Roughening provides an increased surface area which may affect water retention and evaporation rates from the stone surface, influencing biological re-growth. Chemical cleaning may also affect the porosity and permeability of the stone.

Horizontal and sloping masonry and architectural features exposed to more frequent wetting are more susceptible to biological re-growth. The results of cleaning masonry subject to algal growth is sometimes different from that on unaffected stone (Plates 5.10 and 5.11).

It is possible that the rapid colonisation by algae on recently cleaned buildings has been made worse by the decrease in sulphur dioxide present in the atmosphere as a result of the implementation of the Clean Air Act.

Not all biological growth is detrimental to the appearance of masonry, indeed there may be situations where the appearance of older buildings is enhanced by biological growths, particularly lichens. There are however situations where, for aesthetic or maintenance reasons, biological growth needs to be removed.

Plate 5.10 Before cleaning. Typical soiling pattern of sloping stonework. The higher moisture content of the exposed stone has attracted a high degree of soiling and algal growth.

Plate 5.11 After cleaning (same area as Plate 5.10). Note residual soiling reflects the pattern of organic growths prior to cleaning. Areas affected by biological growths are cleaner than those which were unaffected by biological growths.

5.6 Chemical cleaning practice

The range of factors influencing the action of the cleaning chemicals is considerable and many operatives will be unaware of the implications of these interacting factors. For example, the speed of chemical reactions is influenced by the ambient temperature. Higher temperatures increase reaction rates. Manufacturers typically give only general indications of dwell times under cold and warm conditions and the recommended ranges of dwell times may be considerable.

Test panels

If cleaning is contemplated it is recommended that test panels should be cleaned as a pre-contract activity to allow a maximum time for observation of cleaned test panels.

Cleaning of test panels in a variety of situations should be carried out before any decision to clean an entire building is taken (Plate 5.12). The aim of cleaning of test panels should be to establish the minimum concentration of chemicals required for the shortest length of time to effect a level of cleaning consistent with the least damage to the stone. Chapter 6 gives a detailed account of the procedures to be adopted in relation to the chemical cleaning of test panels.

Care needs to be taken when interpreting the results of test panel cleaning. In practice it is often the case that some parts of the building facade clean differently from test panel areas. These include areas which have staining beneath the soiling and those areas subject to more frequent cycles of wetting and drying.

Test panels should be re-inspected at a later date to check for any alteration to their condition over time (e.g. deterioration, efflorescences, algal growth, resoiling and colour change). Ideally, chemically cleaned test panels should be left for as long a time as possible in order to observe these changes. The cautious, patient and wise building owner would wait in excess of a year for these results. In practice, it may not be possible to wait this long. However, it should be remembered that many of the effects of chemical cleaning may not be apparent immediately after cleaning.

It should also be borne in mind that the degree of care and conditions under which the test panels are cleaned may be much better than those which pertain to the cleaning of the rest of the building. The cleaning of a small area of a test panel is much easier to control than that of the entire facade. Dwell time, for example, can be much more closely monitored.

Only after careful analysis of all the information available from the various test panels should any decision about cleaning be taken. Care should be taken to ensure that any cleaning which subsequently takes place is done under the same conditions as the test panels.

Protection of personnel and buildings

Procedures to protect the general public and those carrying out stonecleaning work, the building itself and its environment from any chemical contamination should be in place before any cleaning commences. Suitable protective clothing must be worn by operatives when handling, mixing and rinsing off chemicals. Protective clothing should be washed after use to ensure no residual chemicals remain on clothing. Acidic and alkaline chemical cleaners can cause serious injury in both their liquid and vapour form. Injury can be caused to the skin and eyes and also to the respiratory tract. Adequate first aid equipment should be on site and personnel should be trained in its use. If hydrofluoric acid based chemicals are being used, hydrofluoric acid burn gel must be readily available. The use of chemical cleaners is subject to the Control of Substances Hazardous to Health Regulations 1988 (COSHH) and the Construction Regulations 1961 and 1966.

Those parts of buildings which are not to come into contact with cleaning chemicals (for example glass) should be properly protected by material which will not be attacked by the chemicals (Plate 5.13). Scaffolding should be sheeted to prevent the drift of any airborne chemicals. The ends of scaffolding tubes should be capped to prevent chemical fluids or vapours entering them. Protective sheeting should be designed and applied to the collection and run-off flow of residual chemicals to avoid the risk of concentration and contamination. Chapter 7 provides a summary of the main health and safety regulations which apply to stonecleaning work.

Dilution of chemicals

Reference should always be made to the appropriate health and safety legislation. The manufacturers of stonecleaning chemicals issue general guide-lines on the dilution of their chemicals. Care must be taken to dilute any chemicals in accordance with manufacturers instructions. Ideally concentrated chemicals should not be stored or mixed on site. Chemicals which are supplied in dilute form by the manufacturers reduce the risks involved in handling and mixing. It is advisable to test the effects of varying the concentration of chemicals recommended by manufacturers, on test panels, before application to the whole building. This may involve further dilution to achieve an appropriate working strength.

Environmental concerns

The potential environmental effects of the use of chemicals should be considered. Any regulations regarding the discharge of effluents into the public drainage system need to be checked. Effluent run-off from the building needs to be monitored so as to minimise any local environmental damage. Airborne chemicals can cause damage to people and property (e.g. etching of glass, damage to car paintwork). Solid residues (e.g. poultice) also need to be disposed of so as not to cause problems to public drains.

Plate 5.12 Chemical cleaning test panels. Heavily soiled sloping area has also been test cleaned.

Plate 5.13 Proper protection of areas from which chemicals are to be excluded is essential.

Mortar repairs

In order to prevent excessive amounts of chemicals entering the stonework through open joints and decayed pointing, masonry work should be repaired prior to any chemical cleaning taking place. Failure to do this could lead to efflorescences subsequently developing around the area of the open joint.

Pre-wetting

The chemical cleaning process sometimes begins with the pre-wetting of the area to be cleaned using a cold water jetting procedure. The generally recognised aim of pre-wetting is to remove loose soiling material and prevent the chemicals being drawn too deeply into the masonry by filling the pores of the stone with water. However, the water filled pores may provide a path for easy diffusion of chemicals into the stone. There has been no substantial research investigating whether pre-wetting actually does prevent chemicals from being drawn into the stone. Some small scale testing by Dixon (1993) indicated that, on the sandstone of the Scott Monument in Edinburgh, prewetting the stone would not, in general, slow down the ingress of applied chemicals and, in the case of less permeable stones, penetration could be accelerated. MacDonald and Tonge (1993) found that on ideal, inert, model systems prewetting allowed greater penetration of chemicals from poultices. However, on a real sandstone the differences between dry and pre-wet systems were not so clear cut and active chemicals from a poultice penetrated to approximately the same extent on both wet and dry stones. In the absence of full knowledge the manufacturers guidelines should be followed on practical grounds.

Pre-wetting is generally omitted when cleaning with poultice type systems since the absorption of water from saturated stonework into the poultice would cause the poultice to slough off the surface. Pre-wetting is also omitted when non-aqueous solvents are to be used in cleaning procedures.

Degreasers

Concentrations, dwell times and coverage rates are given by manufacturers for general guidance and should be investigated at the test panel stage. Degreasers are sometimes applied to heavily soiled surfaces before the application of acid cleaning agents. Degreasers assist in softening grease and dirt on the surface of the stone which might otherwise repel the subsequently applied acidic cleaning fluids. They vary in chemical composition but many are alkaline based, containing sodium hydroxide (NaOH). Some degreasers contain a thickening agent designed to aid the adhesion of the degreaser to the surface of the stone.

The use of sodium based degreasers can lead to the formation of soluble salts in stone. The most dangerous of the soluble salts is considered to be sodium sulphate which undergoes a very large volume change when it hydrates. If the salt has been deposited within the pores of a stone, the volume change on hydration generates enormous pressures, more than sufficient to disaggregate the structure of the stone. Schaffer (1932) first drew attention to the dangers of sodium based chemicals and advocated that under no circumstances should they be applied to sandstones. If degreasing of stone is considered to be a necessary pre-requirement to the use of acid based cleaners, alternative degreasers such as detergents, should be tested in any situation in which harmful salts could remain in the stone.

Dwell times for degreasers vary depending on their chemical composition, the nature of stone and the deposits to be softened or removed. Pressure washing is often employed to remove the degreaser from the surface. This process is not always effective in removing these chemicals. In sandstones, significant amounts of degreaser can be retained in the stone (Webster *et al.*, 1992). The extent to which high pressure water washing might force chemical degreasers further into the stone is also unclear.

Degreasers can also take the form of poultices. The degreasing chemical is mixed with clay to form the poultice. The poultice can then be trowelled onto the dry or semi-dry stone to the prescribed depth. Plastic film is placed over the poultice to prevent it from drying out (Plate 5.14). After the necessary dwell time the plastic film is removed and the poultice is scraped off with wooden or plastic scrapers. The residual poultice is then removed by water washing. This may result in soluble chemicals being washed into the pore structure of the stone.

Plate 5.14 Poultice cleaning. Plastic film in place to prevent poultice drying out.

Acid cleaning

Acid based cleaners are normally applied after the degreasing stage. Concentrations, dwell times and coverage rate are given by manufacturers for general guidance and should be investigated at the test panel stage. Great care needs to be taken over these variables, as considerable damage can be done at this stage in the cleaning process. The speed of cleaning reactions is influenced by ambient temperature. It is the temperature of the stonework which is important, not that of the air, since cleaning takes place on the stonework. Manufacturers typically give general indications of dwell times under cold and warm conditions and these can be used for guidance. Stonework temperatures on a given building can vary considerably with weather conditions, with degree of shading and exposure to sunlight. Hence, the procedures adopted as a result of test panel work must be applied with a cautious awareness of the temperature effect.

The area of application of the cleaning agent needs to be considered in advance. Application needs to be even and planned between architectural features. Cleaning should start at the top of the building so that effluent is not washing over previously cleaned areas. Methods for applying chemicals to masonry vary, brushes and low pressure sprays are commonly used. Once the cleaning chemical has been applied, it can be agitated if necessary by brushing the surface of the stone. In practise this type of agitation is sometimes omitted.

Neutralisation

The application of alkaline degreasers often leaves residual alkalinity within stonework. When the degreasing stage is followed by an acid cleaning process the alkalinity is neutralized as a natural consequence. When the cleaning is accomplished by the application of the alkaline degreaser alone an acid treatment is still necessary in order to achieve neutralisation of residual alkalinity. This neutralisation stage generally requires the use of less aggressive, less concentrated acids and shorter dwell times than an acid cleaning process. There may, in practice, be no clear cut distinction between acid cleaning and neutralisation. These may utilise concentrated solutions of aggressive acids with long dwell times at one end (acid cleaning), and dilute solutions of mild acids with short dwell times at the other end (neutralisation).

Washing off

Following a chemical treatment such as degreasing, acid cleaning or neutralisation, thorough washing down of the masonry is very important to remove as much of the cleaning chemicals as possible. This is usually done with a high pressure low volume water lance, although as has already been pointed out, high pressures are probably unnecessary and have the potential to physically damage the stone. In addition high pressure water when directed straight on to masonry can force chemicals more deeply into the stone rather than washed them off. Even after washing down with water, significant amounts of cleaning chemicals may well remain within the stone. Particular attention should be paid to washing down or protecting areas which might trap water, for example recesses and sills.

Ashurst (1988) suggests washing down using a pump producing 20l/min. at 1000psi, rinsing for a minimum of 4 minutes per square metre. This pressure will damage some sandstones and lower pressures may be equally effective.

It is common practice to commence washing off at the base of a facade and in a series of traverses work upwards to the top of the area being cleaned. Since washing takes several minutes per square metre it is clear that this procedure may give significantly greater dwell times to upper areas than lower. The decision on how large an area is to be cleaned at any one time, must take this time factor into account.

Appearance after cleaning

The end result of chemical cleaning is very much dependent on proper examination of the building and stone prior to cleaning along with full testing and the skill of the operative. Chemical cleaning can be very effective at removing soiling (Plates 5.15), however this can have the effect of highlighting residual staining. If proper testing has taken place prior to chemical cleaning no further cleaning should be necessary. In practise stubborn accumulations of soiling are sometimes given a further treatment of acid cleaner, although this can expose the stone to more damage. Careful examination of the building prior to any decision about cleaning may reveal whether residual staining is likely to be a problem. Chemical cleaning can be one cause of stone decay (Plates 5.16 and 5.17). Efflorescences and staining may be particularly marked on stone affected by long term dampness (Plate 5.18 and 5.19). Areas of stonework which are difficult to access with cleaning chemicals, (for example, behind downpipes) may also retain their soiling (Plate 5.20).

Plate 5.15 Contrast between chemically cleaned stone (right) and uncleaned (left) areas of stonework.

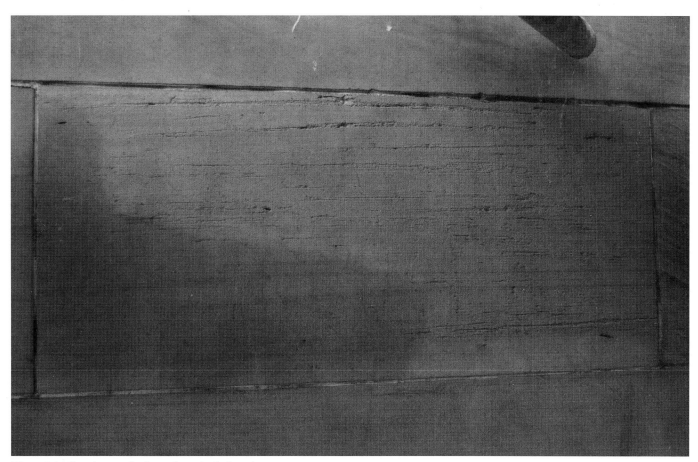

Plate 5.16 Sandstone before chemical cleaning.
Slight decay within particular layers of the sandstone.

Plate 5.17 After chemical cleaning (same area as Plate 5.16).
There has been some further attack on previously decayed layers in the stone. This may be due to chemical attack or be the result of abrasion during the pressure water washing stage of the cleaning process.

Plate 5.18 Area of sandstone before cleaning.
Efflorescence and soiling where stone remained damp for long periods due to a leaking pipe.

Plate 5.19 After chemical cleaning (same area as plate 5.18).
Staining and efflorescences remain in the area affected by long term dampness.

Plate 5.20 After chemical cleaning.
Soiling retained behind a drainage pipe where access by cleaning chemicals was difficult.

Plate 5.21 Before chemical cleaning.
Smooth, vertical sandstone facade soiled by rainwater run-off from ledge below niche.

Plate 5.22 After cleaning (same area as plate 5.21).
Most soiling has been removed by stonecleaning. Some residual soiling remains.

Plate 5.23 Before chemical cleaning. Intense soiling in areas of water run-off.

Plate 5.24 After chemical cleaning (same area as plate 5.23). Some ingrained soiling remains in the area affected by water run-off.

Plate 5.25 After chemical cleaning. Part of this balustrade shows deeply ingrained soiling in an area of very exposed stonework. Such soiling is very difficult or impossible to remove without excessive damage to the fabric of the stone.

Technical problems associated with chemical cleaning

The main technical problems associated with chemical cleaning involve the extent and effects of the retention of chemicals, and the possible mobilisation of salts within the stone. Chemical cleaning can also be problematic in terms of the effects of bleaching and residual staining. Clearly, before any form of chemical cleaning is contemplated, these quite complex phenomena need to be understood in relation to the nature of the stone and the chemicals used. Examples abound of buildings which have been cleaned chemically without due attention to these processes and where, as a result, irreversible damage has been done.

Good cleaning practice

The testing procedures outlined in Chapter 6 should be followed prior to any chemical cleaning. The training, skills and awareness of the operatives are also of vital importance. The potential pitfalls are enormous, and once damage has been done it is impossible to rectify. Attention needs to be paid not only to the short term effects of cleaning, but also to any longer term changes to the stone. Unlike physical cleaning methods, the effects of chemical cleaning may not be immediately apparent. Good cleaning practice requires an understanding of all these processes, and the ability to act responsibly on the basis of that knowledge.

5.7 Summary of chemical cleaning methods

Chemical cleaning methods work by chemical reaction between the cleaning agent, soiling and masonry surface. Many different chemicals are used. Alkalis (commonly sodium hydroxide) or acids (commonly hydrofluoric acid) are frequently used. Alkalis are mainly used as degreasers prior to application of acidic cleaners.

Hydrofluoric acid is capable of dissolving all minerals in stone and can be very damaging if improperly used. Problems include loss of mineral cements, grain loss, surface roughening, pitting, bleaching, staining and deposition of insoluble silica residues. Alteration to the porosity of the stone may also alter susceptibility to algal re-growth following cleaning. Some retained chemicals may act as nutrients to algae and other organisms.

Sandstones may retain a large proportion of the chemicals that are applied to them. Retention of sodium hydroxide may cause particular problems leading to efflorescences and accelerated stone decay as the sodium residues react with pollutants in the stone.

Chemical cleaning can cause staining of stonework by mobilising coloured minerals in the stone and redepositing them on the stone surface. Alternatively, bleaching may result from loss of coloured minerals from the stone.

Given the potential problems of chemical cleaning, its irreversible nature and largely unknown long term effects any decision to clean chemically must be carefully considered.

Chapter 6 Testing methodology

6.1 Testing programme

The testing procedure to be followed before any stonecleaning work is undertaken can be divided into three stages. The first stage involves preliminary examination of the building or facade where cleaning is proposed, identification of stone type and selection of a number of cleaning techniques for testing. In the second stage test panels are cleaned by each of the selected cleaning techniques. The final stage involves analysis and reporting of the results of test cleaning. Once this series of technical steps have been taken and a report produced, a decision can be made as to whether to clean, and which method or methods to use. These technical decisions need to be considered in conjunction with the aesthetic decision checklist (Chapter 3)

6.2 Testing methods

Depth profiling

Depth profiling is a technique which allows the presence of potentially damaging soluble salts in stone or mortar to be measured before and after cleaning, to establish whether or not chemical cleaning has left any residues in the stone. Depth profile testing should always be done when chemical cleaning is being contemplated. The simplest technique uses cores taken from the stone. These must be extracted using a dry coring system, to prevent any redistribution or loss of soluble residues which could occur using a wet coring method.

To obtain a depth profile it is first necessary to establish the sampling intervals which will be measured. With sandstones, useful sampling depths have typically been 0.5 to 2mm intervals to depths of up to, or over, 20mm from the stone face. The soluble salts are extracted into distilled water from rock powder and may be analysed by ion chromatography, atomic absorption spectrophotometry, ICP (inductively coupled plasma emission spectrometry) or any other suitable method.

Two methods have been found to be equally successful for obtaining rock powder for analysis. The first method involves drilling in measured stages to a depth of 2cm using a flat tipped tungsten carbide 10mm diameter drill. At each depth the drill is raised and the finely powdered drillings are collected. Typically samples might be taken every 2mm depending on the stone type. If necessary, drillings can be taken from several locations across the stone if more powder is required for analysis. Successive drillings are made to deeper levels until the total required depth is reached. The second method involves dry sawing the core in successive slices of the required sampling depth. In practice, especially for small sampling intervals, this results in the production of a rock powder rather than a slice of rock. The powder is recovered for analysis. The rock powder from either of these sampling techniques, should not be further milled (i.e. ground to a finer powder) as this could increase extraction of ions from mineral species. It is only the soluble salts in the stone which are required for analysis. This work can be undertaken by some universities and commercial testing laboratories.

Chemical analysis should look for the presence of any ions likely to have been introduced into the stone from the chemical cleaning (e.g. sodium (Na^+), fluorine (F^-), phosphate (PO_4^{3-})) or any other ions which may be present and could form salts harmful to the stone. It is useful to look for sulphate (SO_4^{2-}), which is virtually ubiquitous in the soiling layer on stones and is often mobilised during chemical cleaning. Note that sodium sulphate (Na_2SO_4) can be particularly damaging to stone.

Chemical analysis of efflorescences

Salts differ in their potential to cause stone decay. Efflorescences present before or after cleaning should therefore be analysed in case they prove to be damaging to the stone. If efflorescence is present in sufficient quantities for a sample to be removed, the best method for the identification of salts is by X-ray diffraction (XRD). If the efflorescence occurs in quantities insufficient for (XRD) analysis it should be possible to obtain the chemical composition of the salt using a scanning electron microscope (SEM) capable of elemental X-ray analysis (see below). Alternatively the depth profiling method (above) will indicate which soluble ions are present in the stone.

Petrological analysis

Petrological analysis involves the preparation of thin sections of stone on glass microscope slides. It is most useful to take sections perpendicular to the surface of the stone so that data may be obtained regarding the thickness or penetration of the soiling layer. Observations can also be made of any alteration or weathering in the surface of the stone. In sections taken after cleaning, it may be possible to estimate how much material has been lost from the stone surface. Residues of soiling in the pore spaces between grains could indicate that little or no grain loss has occurred. In chemical cleaning, soluble minerals (e.g. calcite) or softer minerals (e.g. clay) may be lost from near the surface. Alterations to the stone colour may also be visible as zonal changes across the depth of the stone.

The stone should be impregnated with a coloured resin prior to slicing. This has the advantage that it highlights pore spaces and bonds the stone surface which might otherwise be lost during preparation of the thin sections. The thin section is then examined under an optical, polarised light microscope to reveal the stone's mineralogy and structure. Petrological analysis of stone samples carried out in this way will give details of the type and amount of mineral grains and cements in the stone, grain size, shape and sorting, decay or alteration of minerals, the depth and thickness of the soiling layer and a rough estimate of porosity.

Scanning electron microscopy (SEM)

The scanning electron microscope enables examination of an object at a very small scale. Areas as small as a few microns across can be examined and photographed. The technique can only be used on small (approximately 1cm diameter) samples of stone and consequently it is not possible to look at exactly the same area of stone before and after cleaning. With most electron microscopes it is also possible to analyse the chemical elements which are present in a chosen area or mineral grain (e.g. salt crystals could be analysed to reveal their composition). The SEM can be used to look for microscopic changes to the stone surface, for example etching of mineral surfaces, breakage of grains, or precipitation of new minerals.

Surface roughness

Any changes to the surface roughness of stone following cleaning is an important consideration in relation to cleaning decisions, as increased surface roughness leads to slower water run-off from the building facade. Water retention by the stone will be increased, which in turn could increase the rate of stone decay. Increased surface roughness is also likely to increase the resoiling rate and promote algal growth.

Unless samples of stone with the surface intact can be taken for analysis, it is generally only possible to make an assessment of stone roughness by visual observation *in situ*. In some cases surface roughening may be immediately obvious. Lower degrees of roughening can often be detected by touch. It should be noted that if a stone has an obvious fabric (i.e. layering) its roughness may be different across and along the grain.

If samples have been analysed petrographically it may be possible to make some assessment of the amount of surface loss by comparing sections before and after cleaning. If samples of stone can be removed for analysis it is possible to get a quantitative measurement of surface roughness. Form Talysurf is another method used for the measurement of surface roughness. In this method a fine diamond-tipped needle moves over the surface of the stone to give a measure of average surface roughness. As the Form Talysurf method requires stone to be removed for analysis, it is not possible to measure the surface roughness of the same stone sample before and after cleaning. Figure 6.1 gives an example of Form Talysurf analysis.

It may be possible to get useful data by taking an impression of the stone surface using some appropriate material which is pressed onto the stone surface, and using the impression formed for Form Talysurf analysis.

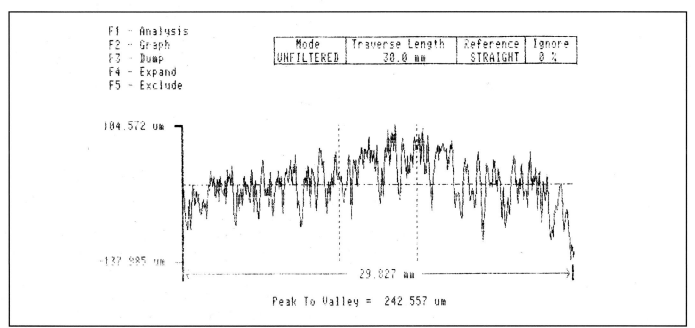

Figure 6.1 Example of Form Talysurf analysis of surface roughness.

Stone porosity

Stone porosity can be measured by mercury porosimetery. This method works by intruding mercury into a stone sample under vacuum. The pressure required to force mercury into the pores is proportional to the entrance diameter of the pores. This gives a measure not only of the effective pore volume of a stone but also the pore size distribution. Testing of stone porosity is expensive and in practice is sometimes omitted.

Stone permeability

It may be useful to obtain data on stone permeability before and after cleaning. Permeability can be easily measured using a simple device in the form of a graduated tube with an open sided, bulbous base. This is attached to the stone face to form a waterproof seal by a ring of non-staining putty like material between the flat, circular brim of the tube and the surface of the stone. On heavily soiled surfaces it may be difficult to achieve a waterproof seal. The tube is designed for application to flat smooth vertical surfaces and measures horizontal transport of water into the stone. After the testing apparatus has been fixed to the surface, water is added through the upper, open end of the pipe until the column reaches the zero graduation mark. The rate of water absorption by the stone can determined by noting the time taken for the water meniscus to pass each graduation mark (e.g. every $0.5cm^3$). The results are presented in the form of the volume of water absorbed over a given time. This measure provides some indication of the stone's resistance to wind-driven rain and other water penetration through the stone surface. Figure 6.2 and Plate 6.1 illustrate the pipe-like apparatus designed for vertical surfaces.

Stones may vary in character from one area of the stone to another so it is important that measurement of absorption rates for comparison purposes before and after cleaning should always be made at the same position on the stone.

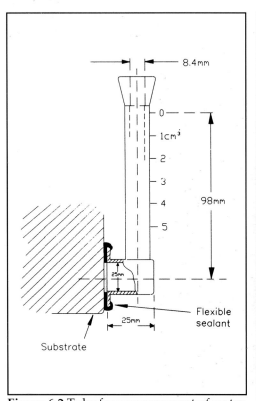

Figure 6.2 Tube for measurement of water absorption rate.

Plate 6.1 Measuring water absorption rate.

100

pH testing

The pH value is used to express the degree of acidity or alkalinity of a solution. A value of 7 is neutral, values below 7 becoming increasingly acidic and values above 7 increasingly alkaline.

Testing of stone pH is conducted before and after chemical cleaning to ensure that neutralization of cleaning agents has taken place. Immediately following the chemical cleaning or poultice treatment, litmus paper is applied to the stone surface while it is in the process of drying out. It may be the case that the stone surface which initially indicates a neutral pH immediately after neutralisation following an alkaline cleaning process, becomes more alkaline in the following minutes. This is due to alkaline chemicals from the degreasing stage diffusing back to the surface of the stone before it dries out. The neutralising chemical should be reapplied until the surface remains neutral to litmus paper.

It should be noted that this will only give an indication of pH at the stone surface. More complex procedures would be required to test pH levels within the stone itself.

Colour testing

Colours can be classified into the three elements of hue, lightness and saturation. Hue refers to colour (e.g. red, blue, yellow), lightness refers to the dimension of brightness and saturation refers to the vividness of the colour, (i.e., dull-bright). Colours can thus be expressed three dimensionally on these three variables. Recently, relatively inexpensive and portable electronic chroma meters have become available which allow the colour of reflected light from masonry to be quickly and accurately measured (Plate 6.2). These machines offer the possibility of monitoring the colour of masonry much more effectively than has been possible in the past and this has a significant value for stonecleaning practitioners. Acceptable colour ranges for cleaned stonework could, for example, form part of a stonecleaning contract. Colour testing should always be carried out when the masonry is dry, as wet stonework is significantly different in colour from dry stonework.

Plate 6.2 Testing stone colour using a portable chroma meter.

6.3 Testing procedure

Stage 1: Preliminary examination

The aim of the preliminary visual examination is to provide a detailed site assessment of the building or facade to be cleaned, noting soiling level and distribution patterns, stonework defects, variations in stone type, geometry, micro-climatic effects and any other factors (e.g. poor or inadequate maintenance) which could affect cleaning or the subsequent weathering of the building, should it be cleaned.

Procedure

A systematic examination should be made of the whole area of stonework to be cleaned, taking photographs where appropriate. Current defects on the facade such as spalling, stone deterioration, decayed mortar joints, areas of biological growth and staining of the stone should be identified. Any efflorescences present should be noted and samples may be taken for analysis. Any variations in surface texture and architectural decoration, which could affect the choice of stonecleaning method, should be noted. The number of different stone types and any variants of particular stone types need to be recorded. The pattern and variations in soiling level across the building should be considered, as this could affect the method of stonecleaning chosen. Micro-climatic variations should be detailed. The prevailing air currents around a building and the pattern of water run-off from the surface can affect the way in which soiling is distributed on the masonry. It is often the case that areas of heavy soiling clean differently to lightly soiled areas. Much of this information could be recorded on architectural drawings, photographs or sketches of the building facade.

The end result of this preliminary investigation should be a detailed account of the facade, noting those features which could affect any decisions regarding stonecleaning. It may be possible, at this stage, to rule out some stonecleaning methods from further consideration.

On the basis of the evidence gathered from the preliminary examination, a decision will be taken as to whether to proceed with the cleaning of test panels, and if so which stonecleaning methods are to be tested.

Stage 2: Cleaning test panels

If the decision is taken to proceed further, locations need to be selected for the test panels for each of the stonecleaning methods to be considered. These test panels (normally up to 1m^2) should be on representative areas of each stone type, preferably on unobtrusive parts of the building. Test panels are sometimes inappropriately selected simply on the basis of access, and then usually only on areas relatively easy to clean such as flat, vertical faces of the facade. A more representative test is recommended and should include recessed or more complex areas where the soiling accumulation will be different to that on the vertical facade. It may also be necessary to test clean areas of different surface texture, degree of decay or any other variations present on the facade. Field observations suggest that in some situations the number of test panels on buildings escalates enormously. If a subsequent decision not to clean is taken, these test panels can be visually detrimental.

Procedures for the monitoring of test panels using physical and chemical cleaning techniques differ slightly. The detailed procedures to be carried out on test panels for each cleaning method are therefore dealt with separately. The procedures outlined represent a comprehensive range of tests which would ideally be carried out. In some situations some of these tests are omitted. With chemical cleaning trials the most important information is likely to come from depth profiles taken from core samples. The depth of penetration, amount and nature of any salts present within the stone will be important information on which to base any decision on chemical cleaning. In terms of physical cleaning trials, damage to the stone surface or mortar and changes in surface roughness which could lead to increased water absorbency will be important information. Some stonecleaning contractors may not themselves be able to carry out the full range of scientific tests recommended. Facilities for carrying out these tests are available from specialist laboratories and some universities.

There are some situations where some, or all, cleaning methods may be ruled out at an early stage. Some indications of where chemical or physical cleaning methods are likely to be inappropriate are given below.

Inappropriate chemical cleaning situations

Hydrofluoric acid (HF) based cleaners or other corrosive chemicals must never be used on highly polished stone. Care should be taken if there is polished stone in the vicinity of chemical cleaning activity, as even wash-off water which spills on to polished surfaces can be damaging. Chemical cleaning is inappropriate in any situation where materials which might be affected cannot be adequately protected.

High pressure water jetting as part of a chemical or physical cleaning procedure can be highly damaging to soft or decayed stone.

Chemical retention is likely to be high on very porous stone or stone with a high clay content (e.g. mudstone and some sandstones).

Chemical retention is also likely to be high on highly weathered or decayed stone and cleaning of such stonework can often cause extensive loss of stone surface.

Calcareous stones are highly susceptible to acid based cleaners which can rapidly dissolve the cementing minerals in the stone. Dilute hydrochloric acid can be used on site to test for calcareous sandstones. If, on application of a small quantity of hydrochloric acid, the stone effervesces, then the sandstone is calcareous and acid based cleaners should not be used.

Where there are open joints in the stonework chemicals will be able to penetrate the joints very deeply and are likely to be difficult or impossible to remove from these areas.

Poultices may be difficult to remove from carved or intricate areas of stonework.

Inappropriate physical cleaning situations

Grit blasting methods should never be used on highly polished stone.

Harsh abrasive methods should not be used on delicately carved stonework, or smooth ashlar if its use would lead to excessive surface roughening.

Abrasive methods (including high pressure water jetting) may be highly damaging to softer or decayed stone.

Test panel cleaning

These suggested procedures should represent a very comprehensive analysis of test panel cleaning. In some situations not all these tests might be considered necessary. The minimum which should be undertaken in relation to chemical cleaning would be depth profile analysis, and analysis of surface roughness and erosion of detailing in relation to physical cleaning.

Test panels: Chemical cleaning

The aim of test cleaning should be to establish the minimum necessaary chemical concentrations and dwell times.

Before test cleaning

All procedures should be recorded and photographed in detail. An example of a data recording log is given in Figure 6.3.

1. Assess the state of the stone and mortar in detail with particular reference to:

- Decay
- Soiling level
- Colour
- Surface roughness
- Presence of efflorescences (take samples for analysis)
- Presence of biological growths

2. Undertake on-site trials or take stone samples or cores for the following analyses (see Section 6.2 Testing methods):

- Depth profiling
- Petrographic analysis
- Microscopic surface examination by scanning electron microscope (SEM)
- Stone porosity
- Stone permeability
- pH of stone surface

3. Proceed with test cleaning in accordance with the guidance previously given, recording process in detail.

Immediately after test cleaning

1. Assess in detail the state of the stone and mortar with reference to:

- Any loss, damage or alteration to the stone or mortar
- Residual soiling
- Colour (including presence of any bleaching or staining)
- Surface roughness
- Efflorescences (take samples for analysis)
- Stone permeability
- pH of stone surface
- Any residues of cleaning materials

2. Take stone or core samples for the following analyses:

- Depth profiling
- Petrographic analysis
- SEM examination of surface

At a later date after cleaning

After a period of time has elapsed following cleaning (up to a year), the test panels need to be reassesed for changes which may have taken place since the initial examination immediately after cleaning.

1. Record changes to:

- State of decay of stone and mortar
- Soiling level
- Colour
- Surface roughness
- Efflorescences (take samples for analysis)
- Presence of biological soiling

2. Take further stone or core samples adjacent to the original locations for the following analysis:

- Depth profiling

Test panels: Physical cleaning

The aim of test cleaning should be to establish the minimum blasting or washing pressures necessary to achieve a satisfactory level of cleaning with minimal damage to the stone.

Before test cleaning

All procedures should be recorded and photographed in detail. An example of a data recording log is given in Figure 6.4.

1. Assess the state of the stone and mortar in detail with particular reference to:

- Decay
- Soiling level
- Colour
- Surface roughness
- Presence of efflorescences (take samples for analysis)
- Presence of biological growths

2. Undertake on-site trials or take stone samples or cores for the following analyses:

- Petrographic analysis
- Microscopic surface examination by SEM
- Stone permeability

3. Proceed with test cleaning in accordance with the guidance previously given, recording process in detail

Immediately after test cleaning

1. Assess in detail the state of the stone and mortar with reference to:

- Any loss, damage or alteration to the stone or mortar
- Residual soiling
- Colour
- Surface roughness
- Any residues of cleaning materials

2. Undertake on-site trials or take stone samples or cores for the following analyses:

- Petrographic analysis
- Microscopic surface examination by SE
- Stone permeability

Stage 3: Reporting results of test cleaning

After the cleaning of the test panels and the completion of the various scientific tests, evaluation of all the available information can proceed.

This should begin with a visual examination of the test panels noting the extent to which biological and non-biological soiling has been removed. The extent and location of any residual soiling or efflorescences should be assessed taking into account its effect on the appearance of the facade. Any bleaching or staining, whether from the cleaning process itself or revealed following the removal of soiling, should be noted. An examination should also be made of any visible changes to the surface texture of the stone, including loss of weathered or decayed areas of stone or loss of surface patina. The effects of the cleaning process on the mortar should also be noted.

Results from the various scientific tests carried out on the stone need to be considered along with the visual data from the test panels. A comprehensive report (including photographic documentation where appropriate) covering the results of the examination and scientific testing procedures in stages 1 and 2 should be prepared. Any changes that may have occurred in the period following cleaning should also be documented. This is especially important where chemical cleaning has been carried out as efflorescence may take some days or weeks to become visible.

This report should provide conclusions detailing the proposed intentions and prescriptive specification of the method or methods to be adopted. Evaluation should always be approached on a damage limitation basis, if doubt persists, the option not to clean should be considered.

Figure 6.3 Chemical cleaning data recording log

Stonecleaning operations : Chemical methods	
Location :	Date :
Panel / sample / building :	Wash-off temperature :
Cleaned by :	Type of chemical :
Prewash? :	Method of application :
Prewash pressure :	Time in contact with stone :
Prewash temperature :	Method of removal :
Type of chemical :	Wash-off pressure :
Method of application :	Wash-off temperature :
Time in contact with stone :	pH of stone before/after :
Method of removal :	Weather conditions :
Wash-off pressure :	Samples taken? :
Stone description :	
Photo numbers :	
Notes :	

Figure 6.4 Physical cleaning data recording log

Stonecleaning operations : Physical methods

Location :	
Panel / sample / building :	
Cleaned by :	
Grit type :	
Wet or dry :	
Pressure :	
Water temperature :	
Water supply rate :	
Time taken for cleaning :	
Nozzle distance :	
Nozzle type :	
Date :	
Wash-off? :	
Wash-off pressure :	
Wash-off temperature :	
Time taken for wash-off :	
Nozzle distance :	
Nozzle type :	
Weather conditions :	
Samples taken? :	
Stone description :	
Photo numbers :	
Notes :	

Chapter 7   Health and safety

7.1 Health and safety considerations

Legislation

Whichever cleaning method is specified or selected, all parties involved in the project, owners, clients, professional advisers, main contractor, sub-contractors and operatives, have certain responsibilities and duties placed on them by the Health and Safety at Work Act 1974, and other relevant legislation.

Under the Act employers have a general duty to ensure, so far as is reasonably practicable, the health, safety and welfare at work of their employees and, where appropriate, non-employees. This duty includes the provision of safe plant and equipment, a safe work place, and all the necessary information, instruction, training and supervision. In addition, employers should consult safety representatives appointed by recognised trade unions.

The employer is also required to prepare and issue a statement of safety policy, when employing five or more employees, outlining the arrangements he is making to satisfy these duties, including how they intend to ensure that the necessary safeguards are adopted. The contractor should be asked by those managing the project to provide a copy of the safety policy, with evidence of ability to put it into practice.

In addition to those directly employed, the employer must ensure, so far as is reasonably practicable, that persons not in his employment are safe and without risk to health, and to provide such information as is necessary to avoid risks. In stonecleaning projects such persons would include occupiers of the premises, visitors to sites and premises and any member of the public who might be affected by the work activities.

Employees have a duty under the Act to take reasonable care of their own safety and the safety of others who may be affected by their actions. They should co-operate with their employer so far as it is necessary to enable their employer to comply with the Act. Every self-employed person is required to conduct their undertaking so as to ensure that they and other people who might be affected are not exposed to risks to their health and safety.

Duties are also imposed on those who have to any extent, control over non-domestic premises which are used by people (not their employees) as a place of work or as a place where they may use machinery, equipment, etc, or substances which have been provided for their use.

The person having any control over the premises, the means of access, or of any plant or substance in the premises, has a duty to ensure that so far as reasonably practicable, they are safe and without risks to health.

Any person who has, through a contract or tenancy, an obligation of any extent in relation to maintenance or repair of the premises or the means of access, or for guarding against hazards from the plant or substances there, will be regarded as the person who has control of the premises, and who has the above duty to the extent of their obligations.

Manufacturers, which means any person or company who designs, makes or supplies (including hiring) anything for use at work, are required to ensure that the product is safe and without risk to health when properly used. This requires paying attention to design and arranging for any necessary testing. Importantly, it also means that users are entitled to necessary information concerning the proper use and any other conditions required to ensure safety and absence of risk to health in connection with the use of the product at work.

The requirements of the Act and related legislation are in their respective spheres enforced by the Health & Safety Executive, certain local authorities and other agents acting on behalf of HSE. The methods of enforcement available to the authorities include prohibition and improvement notices and prosecution. As enforcing authorities they provide advice and information, as well as taking enforcement action when necessary.

Risk assessments

The recently introduced Management and Safety at Work Regulations set out broad duties which apply to most work activities. They are aimed mainly at improving health and safety management and make more explicit what is required under the Health and Safety at Work Act.

Central to the regulations is the requirement on all employers and self employed persons to assess the risks to employees and others who may be affected by their work activities, and the making of arrangements for putting into practice any health and safety measures that may follow from the risk assessment. A record of the assessment must be made if the employer has five or more employees.

The ultimate purpose of the Risk Assessment is to identify any measure an employer may need to effect in order to meet the requirements of any statutory provisions relating to the particular hazard noted. Trivial risks, or those arising from everyday life can usually be ignored, unless the latter are exacerbated by the work process.

Work at heights

Most cleaning projects will involve work at heights with access provided by some type of scaffolding or mobile work platforms. Having selected the system to be used, considerations at the design stage will be influenced by the site location, public access, method selected for cleaning, containment sheeting, lifting operations, loading of the scaffold and site security. In certain chemical applications the ends of scaffold poles must be plugged to prevent ingress of chemicals.

The construction of all scaffolds must be carried out within the requirements of the Construction (Working Places) Regulations 1966 and any local authority requirements. All scaffolds including mobile towers require to be of sound construction and erected, maintained and inspected by a competent person. Where scaffolds are provided by the main contractor for common use, the onus is on the user to ensure that it is fit for its intended use by his employees.

Scaffolds should be inspected weekly to see that they remain in a safe condition and in compliance with the regulations, with details of inspections recorded in the Scaffold Register Form 91.

Scaffolding must be erected on a safe foundation (sole and base plates) and it should be perpendicular without the uprights leaning away from the building. It must be suitably braced and tied and all components properly spaced. The working platforms must be fully boarded out (3 board minimum) and must always be with toeboards and guardrails, with brickguards and containment sheeting fitted where necessary. The access ladders must project 1.0m above the landing platform, should be angled 4:1 to the vertical and should be securely tied.

In certain circumstances, the need for mobile scaffolds may arise. They must be of sound construction, never be less than 1200mm minimum base dimension and the height limitations are $3\frac{1}{2}$ times the shorter base dimension for internal work and 3 times the same dimension for external work, (these dimensions are inclusive of outriggers). Mobile scaffolds should, where possible, be tied into the building. The working platform must be fully boarded and equipped with toeboards, guardrails and an internal secured ladder. The wheels should not be less than 125mm in diameter, they must be secured to the standards and fitted with brakes. Mobile scaffolds should only be used on level, firm ground and must never be moved until all persons have moved to ground level.

Mobile work platforms are sometimes used to provide temporary working places, giving access to localised areas above and below ground level. They provide an alternative to scaffolding and must be used in accordance with the manufacturer's and other guidance.

Hazardous substances

The Control of Substances Hazardous to Health Regulations 1988 (COSHH) define in general and specific terms how employers are expected to safely manage the use of potentially harmful substances.

The Regulations require employers to make an assessment of all work which is liable to expose any employee and other persons to a substance hazardous to health. Most chemical and physical cleaning methods on masonry surfaces require to be assessed as they involve the use of hazardous solids, liquids, dusts, fumes or vapours depending on the method selected.

Managing hazardous substances and complying with the requirements of the COSHH Regulations, requires:-

1. Identification of the hazardous substance involved.

2. Assessment of the risk to health arising from the work and identification of precautions necessary.

3. The introduction of appropriate measures to prevent or control the risk.

4. Checks to ensure that control measures are used and that equipment is properly maintained and procedures observed.

5. Where necessary, exposure to be monitored to ensure that methods and control measures work.

6. Employees to be informed, instructed and trained about the risks and the precautions to be taken.

Assessment means evaluating the risks to health and then deciding on a course of action needed to remove or reduce the risks with the details recorded in writing. The responsibility for assessment should be allocated to a competent person who is adequately trained with access to appropriate levels of advice and professional support as required.

Guidance Note EH40 from the Health & Safety Executive lists the occupational exposure limits which should be used in determining the adequacy of control of exposure by inhalation, as required by the COSHH Regulations.

Persons managing the site/contract have a responsibility to ensure that contractors and others have adequate information to safely plan their work. There is also a responsibility to ensure that they have carried out their COSHH assessments, that they are adequate and have in place a management system for checking on the suitability of the assessments for the work being carried out and to ensure that precautions and controls are being implemented.

The use of masonry biocides are also covered by the above Regulations with approval for use made under the Control of Pesticides Regulations. An Approved Code of Practice has been prepared on "The safe use of pesticides for non-agricultural purposes" which provides practical guidance on the COSHH Regulations as they apply to pesticides in such situations.

Noise

Noise from construction sites is subject to The Control of Pollution Act 1974 (COPA) and the Noise at Work Regulations for employees. The COPA is enforced by the Local Authority who may serve a notice on the contractor specifying the manner in which the work is to be carried out. The purpose of the notice is to provide protection against noise for other people who live or work in the area. The notice may impose constraints on the machinery used, limit work hours or specify acceptable levels of noise. Application for prior consent can be made to the Local Authority with proposals to minimise noise on site. Consent, when given, will greatly reduce the likelihood of such problems, but not altogether eliminate the risk.

The Noise at Work Regulations require employers to assess the risks whenever they reach the "Action Levels" defined in the Regulations, and implement appropriate control measures.

Electricity

The Electricity at Work Regulations 1989 apply to construction sites, and place duties on contractors, employees and the self-employed in so far as they relate to matters which are within their control.

They require the electrical system to be sound, properly installed and maintained (the installation standards set out in the IEE Regulations for Electrical Installations are considered acceptable in this respect). The IEE Regulations set down all the requirements to follow regarding protective devices, cable sizes, etc. These form the basis for any electrical system and do not vary whether the installation is permanent or temporary. They also refer to British Standards and BS 7375 Code of Practice for "Distribution of Electricity on construction and building sites" provides further guidance on the type of electrical apparatus and wiring for site installations.

All persons carrying out electrical work must be competent to do so and expert advice should be sought in order to establish satisfactory arrangements for inspection and maintenance.

Contractual arrangements

Contractual arrangements will have an important bearing on how statutory health and safety responsibilities are managed and discharged. It should define how the parties involved should fulfil their requirements, and will fill out the particulars of the general statutory arrangements for provision of accommodation, welfare facilities, first aid, fire prevention, protective clothing, reporting and recording of accidents, etc.

Proper planning for health and safety should be an integral part of the overall preparation for the efficient running of the project.

Although it is difficult, it is important that consideration for such work should only involve contractors who are able to demonstrate their competency in management of health and safety matters.

New legislation

Currently at the consultation stage with a planned introduction date of 1 October 1994, are the Construction (Design and Management) Regulations, to comply with EEC Directives.

The Regulations will affect cleaning projects and impose new duties upon clients, designers and contractors which will require them to re-think their traditional roles in construction work.

Its aims are to improve co-ordination between the parties involved in construction work at the preparation stage and during work. It does this by assuming the existence of a client for each project, and a project supervisor, either of which appoints co-ordinators for preparation and execution stages of the project. It then requires the co-ordinators to prepare and adjust a safety plan for the project. Everyone involved in the construction process is required to take into account the general principles of prevention and protection which are spelt out in the Framework Directive. Finally, the Directive requires the preparation of a health and safety file about the project itself, which is to be passed on to the client.

Summary

This chapter has attempted to summarise some points which need to be addressed on such projects, but is unable to provide complete coverage of all aspects, and attention is drawn to relevant legislation, COP's and guidance from HSE and others in relation to health and safety.

A useful reference manual which explains the above statutory requirements in more detail is the "Construction Safety" manual published by the Building Advisory Service.

Health and safety information

The Health and Safety at Work etc. Act 1974.
Her Majesty's Stationery Office (HMSO) ISBN 0-10-543774-3

The Control of Substances Hazardous to Health Regulations 1988.
HMSO ISBN 0-11-885468-2

Approved Code of Practice (COSHH Regulations) "The safe use of pesticides for non-agricultural purposes".
HMSO ISBN 0-11-885673-1

The Control of Pesticides Regulations 1986.
HMSO ISBN 0-11-067510-X

Guidance Note EH40 Occupational Exposure Limits 1993.
HMSO ISBN 0-11-882080-X

Electricity at Work Regulations 1989.
HMSO ISBN 0-11-09663-X

Institution of Electrical Engineers Regulations for Electrical Installation (16th Edition).
The Institute of Electrical Engineers

Code of Practice for the Prevention of Fire on Construction Sites.
The Loss Prevention Council ISBN 0-902167-20-0

Managing health and safety in construction: Principals and application to main contractor/subcontractor projects. CONIAC.
HMSO ISBN 0-11-883918-7

The Control of Pollution Act 1974.
HMSO

Proposals for Construction (Design and management) Regulations and Approved Code of Practice. (Draft Document for consultation)

Construction Safety Manual.
The Builders Employers Confederation ISBN 1-85263-002-7

Management of Health and Safety at Work
HMSO ISBN 0-11-886330-4

Noise at Work Regulations
HMSO ISBN 0-11-097790-4

Chapter 8   Planning

8.1 Planning permission

The need for planning

This chapter is intended as a guide to planning authorities in relation to their need to properly record both proposals for stonecleaning and the results of cleaning. Building owners must consult with planning authorities and must recognise their responsibilities with regard to current legislation.

In Scotland, until the Town and Country Planning (General Permitted Development) (Scotland) Order 1992 came into force in March 1992, the requirement to obtain listed building consent for stonecleaning was not clearly stated in the planning legislation. Prior to that date, the decision as to whether or not consent was required rested with the planning authority. Only if the proposed cleaning might "affect the character of the building" would an application for consent be sought. The wording, "affect the character", left some doubt as to whether the authority was obliged to consider the likelihood of either immediate or long-term damage to the stonework as a result of the proposed cleaning. To avoid further doubt and encourage greater thought being given to stonecleaning proposals, the order clearly states (in Class 9 of Part 2 (Sundry Minor Operations) of Schedule 1 (Classes of Permitted Development) that stonecleaning is not permitted development where the building is listed or within a conservation area. As a result of the order, all proposals to stoneclean listed buildings now require listed building consent or, in the case of unlisted buildings within a conservation area, planning permission.

Planning authorities are in a unique position to improve the state of knowledge relating to the best practice for the cleaning of buildings and monuments in their area by developing and maintaining a database on the buildings and their cleaning history. If such records are kept and adequately cross-referenced, this will, in future, greatly increase the possibility of more accurately forecasting the likely results of cleaning, and so aid the decision making process.

The acceptability of any proposal to clean a building can only be determined following a full assessment of the level of risk involved and of the type and extent of damage which may result. The aim must always be to restrict consent to those proposals which, on the basis of recent research and current technical knowledge, reduce to an absolute minimum the risk and possible scale of damage.

It is recommended that the cleaning of any stone building (not just listed buildings) should be a notifiable operation, and that planning permission be required prior to any work being carried out. This may require authorities to consider the adoption of Article 4 procedures in relation to stonecleaning operations. Such a procedure is considered essential if any control is to be maintained and adequate records kept.

Planning considerations

The first question to be asked is, does the building need cleaning? Many buildings are pleasantly weathered giving them an aesthetic quality which stonecleaning would destroy. Chapter 3 gives some guidance on this. In addition, stonecleaning exposes the building to damage from the cleaning process and possible accelerated decay. It must also be remembered that the effects of cleaning may be short term. As a result of increased water absorption, cleaned facades may, in a matter of months, show signs of accelerated surface recolonisation by algal growths, particularly after chemical cleaning. Parts of the building which may be subject to rapid recolonisation by algae may also resoil quickly. However, in some situations stonecleaning may have a beneficial effect in aesthetic and psychological terms.

An applicant should always be advised that cleaning may reveal plastic repairs, indents and pointing, the colour of which was specifically selected to match that of the soiled stonework. Where a cleaning proposal is acceptable in principle it is important that, before consent is given, the applicant should confirm that such work, if found, will be removed and replaced with correctly coursed and pointed indents in carefully matched natural stone and without further damage to the adjacent masonry.

Thought must also be given to where to start, and stop, cleaning. Legal boundaries between properties frequently determine the extent of the proposed work but these may bear little relationship to the external architectural form and detailing of the building. A piecemeal approach to cleaning a property in several different ownerships or one which forms part of a larger block, such as a terrace, will inevitably produce a patchwork effect because of differences in specification and time delays between individual cleaning contracts. The patchwork will significantly affect the architectural integrity of the building or larger block and may become more marked over time as areas of stone cleaned in different ways and at different dates weather and resoil at different rates. Even where cleaning can be justified on architectural grounds, poor workmanship and inadequate supervision of chemical applications can cause serious problems to adjacent properties as a result of wind-drift, spillage and over-application.

Cleaning should never, but all too frequently does, take place where the precise nature of what is to be cleaned and its possible response to the method and materials to be used are not fully understood. Proposals to clean should, therefore, be based upon and supported by analysis of the geological make-up and present condition of the surface of the stone and of the effect that various cleaning processes may have upon these. The onus should be firmly upon the applicant to satisfy the planning authority that it is in the best interests of the building to clean and that the methods and materials to be used will prolong, and not reduce, its life. Where there is any doubt about the basis of a cleaning proposal consent should not be given.

Applicants should be reminded that many of the problems which arise during or after cleaning are a direct consequence of the process of tendering for the work. Often the choice of contractor is determined by the lowest tender price, without the possible implications of such a decision being taken into account. Reputable stonecleaning companies, which are likely to devote time, care and resources to the contract, will be unable to match the price of the many operators offering cheap work who have little or no previous experience of stonecleaning or masonry conservation.

There will be cases where stonework should, under no circumstances, be subject to possible damage. Planning authorities are advised to have a policy which clearly states where cleaning shall and shall not be viewed favourably. Particular care needs to be taken where the stone has a high iron content, where a building displays large areas of high quality architectural detail, sculpture or other decorative work or where the surface to be cleaned forms only part of a single building or of a group of buildings which form an architectural unit. In addition, chemical cleaners should not be used on or near ceramic detail, polished granite and marble as they will remove the surface finish. The policy should also make clear that one cleaning method may not be acceptable for use over a whole building, and that parts of the structure, especially those which are richly decorated, may, because of their form or type of stone, require special treatment. If different stonecleaning techniques are used on a building, careful consideration of the consequences needs to be given. Different stonecleaning techniques can, for example, result in the removal of differing amounts of soiling and variations in the colour of cleaned stone. The rate of resoiling rates can also be influenced by the type of cleaning method used.

Applications are now being made to clean again buildings which have resoiled after the original cleaning. Proposals for work which would repeat or reinforce any of the visual or physical problems created by inappropriate earlier work should not, under any circumstances, be given consent. Detailed research will be required before the reasons for and solutions to each particular problem can be put forward. An increasing number of buildings which are now being proposed for recleaning also require major repairs. Work which may be necessary as a result of accelerated decay promoted by previous stone cleaning requires very careful thought. Each case will be different and solutions must be based upon a full understanding of both the natural and enforced erosion cycles which have occurred since cleaning and of the relationship between these. Owners faced with such repair work should seek guidance from experienced masonry conservators. It should, however, be borne in mind that a building which needs repairs does not, as a matter of course, also require cleaning.

Cleaned buildings may attract graffiti. Some chemicals used in paints are extremely difficult to remove from any porous wall surface as they can penetrate deeply into the stone. There is at present no method of removal which may be used without risk of damaging the stone, especially where the frequency of application of graffiti necessitates repeated treatment. Preventative measures, such as railings or security floodlighting, may eliminate or cut down the problem, and may have to be considered where graffiti and the potential physical damage to masonry caused by its repeated removal cannot be accepted.

Despite detailed research and a much improved state of knowledge regarding the various techniques which may be adopted, there are at present no immediate answers to many of the problems to which stonecleaning may give rise. Cleaning is always undertaken at some risk and many owners are now having to pay out large sums of money to make good damage which is the direct result of badly specified or executed work carried out in the past. Proposals to stoneclean, if they are acceptable in principle and accord with stated policy, must, therefore, be considered with extreme care. It is also important that cleaning should not be permitted unless there is a willingness on the part of the applicant to carry out associated repair work which fulfils the basic maintenance and conservation requirements of the property.

8.2 Stonecleaning applications

To enable an initial assessment of the potential risks of cleaning to be made it is suggested that the applicant should be asked to submit a full survey of the fabric of the building which identifies the stone or stones used and the extent and nature of current defects. Consideration of the stone type should indicate which cleaning methods might be acceptable. The applicant should then be requested to carry out fully monitored trials on small, inconspicuous areas of stonework and submit a detailed report illustrated with photographs. Chapter 6 gives details of these procedures. The number and location of the trial panels should be carefully chosen to ensure that all forms and types of stonework are tested. In some instances further trials of other methods or of the same methods at a later date may be necessary before a final decision can be reached. If any doubts remain, cleaning should not be given consent. Where cleaning is permissible the applicant should be strongly advised, or in the case of buildings of particular architectural or townscape importance perhaps required, to employ contractors of proven ability who are known to be able to carry out the work exactly as specified and with good supervision.

The criteria against which a planning authority will wish to judge any stonecleaning proposal will include:

1. The national and local significance of the building or monument, its history, its listed status, and its importance with regard to any relevant provision of the Development Plan or any other non-statutory policy guidance.

2. The importance of the building's setting in relation to its context; this would consider, amongst other matters, whether it forms a part of an architectural composition such as a street or square, or whether it is a prominent landmark.

3. The potential new uses for the building and the area which might stem from an enhancement of the building.

4. The intensity of soiling of the building, and the likely time cycle of re-soiling.

5. The consequences of the cleaning method proposed for the architecture of the building in question.

Consideration of the implications of this last criterion is likely to be a primary factor in the decision making process and, therefore, it is essential that a database of information relating to previous stonecleaning projects is constantly maintained, updated and intelligently interrogated.

Stonecleaning data base

Planning authorities should set up data bases in which to hold information of stonework and reports produced prior to cleaning and obtained, where cleaning is permitted, during and after the carrying out of the work. This will enable authorities gradually to build up a store of knowledge which will help them to assess the potential damage when an application is submitted during or after cleaning.

Pre-cleaning records

Information which should be recorded and kept on file before cleaning commences should include:

1. The building's address, the date that it was built, its architects and builder if known, and its original, current and proposed use.

2. Relevant background data, such as the level of atmospheric pollution, its proximity to main roads or industrial complexes, etc.

3. A dated photographic record to enable a comparison to be made at a later date and to assist in assessing the time cycle of soiling. The record should include:

   (a) Photographs of the building in context, e.g. its relationship to a larger architectural composition such as a street.

   (b) Photographs of the whole facade(s) to be cleaned, with details of heavily soiled areas and damaged stone. These photographs may have to be at a scale of 1 sq m per 10"x8" print, to provide sufficient information of areas of special importance or concern. Particular attention should be paid to carved ornaments, (all of which should be recorded) and to defects and endemic stains which may be highlighted by cleaning.

   (c) A record of the colour value of the stone, so that colour changes after cleaning may be noted. A relatively simple and accurate technique here is the use of a chromameter, which is held up to the face of the stone and digitally records the colour and brightness. Alternatively, though less satisfactory, a Kodak colourstrip can be photographed beside the stone, and when processed subsequent prints can be adjusted so that the colourstrips all have the same colour value, and the stone colours can consequently be compared, (although there is likely to be a difference between this and the true colour of the stone).

   (d) The mineralogy of the stone must be established and recorded, as it is impossible to predict results in ignorance of the nature of the stone. Thin sections for microscopic examination must be prepared from core samples or available pieces of stone, taken from various positions in the facade, as the stone characteristics are likely to vary. The position on the facade from which the samples have been taken should be recorded in addition to the results of any analysis. The particular qualities of the stone's mineralogy are relevant to the method of cleaning proposed, and the planning authority will have to satisfy itself that the considerations relating to the cleaning of different types of stone are duly taken into account.

(e)The surface texture of the stone should be recorded. This will assist in establishing any differences in the roughness of the stone after cleaning, which may provide a key for soiling or algae growth.

(f)Sample panels should be established for proposed cleaning techniques, and photographic, core samples and surface texture data recorded.

Post-cleaning records

If it is proposed to proceed with cleaning, the method of cleaning actually used must be recorded in detail. The following may form an appropriate check list:-

1. Physical cleaning

Wet or dry grit blast or other abrasive techniques.
Pressures used.
Size and nature of grit/abrasive particles.
Date of operation.

2. Chemical cleaning

The nature and concentration of the chemicals used and the form of their application (e.g. liquid or gel), trade names, etc.
Application areas and dwell times.
Wash off procedures.
Pressure of wash off water.
Weather conditions including ambient temperatures, date of operations.

3. Stone replacements

Repairs and indents should be recorded on a scaled drawing with accompanying photographs.

After cleaning, a detailed photographic record as set out in Pre-cleaning records, Section 3, should be repeated, and notes made regarding residual soiling levels, and the perceived success or otherwise of the operation.

The maintenance of such a database for all buildings will create a record of cleaning operations and enable an assessment of the time cycle of resoiling and associated problems to be made. Future advice will be able to be more soundly based on experience, upon which an appropriate and coherent policy for stonecleaning in the area can be formulated.

Authorities may require evidence of the type set out in pre-cleaning records to be submitted before considering an application; with grant approval being conditional on a detailed record being carried out as described. It is recognised that the cost of making these detailed records may not be feasible for all buildings. Where buildings are not exceptional in any way and where there is clear and satisfactory precedent of successful cleaning of the same stone on similar buildings, a photographic record together with a detailed description of the cleaning method used as set out above may be considered sufficient. Stonecleaning should always be approached on a damage limitation basis, if doubts persist, the option not to clean should be considered.

References

Agarossi, G., Ferrari, R. and Monte, M. 1985, "Microbial biodeterioration in the hypogea: The subterranean neo-pythagorean basilica of Porta Maggiore in Rome", Proceedings of the 5th Intermnational Congress on Deterioration and Conservation of Stone, Lausanne, **2**, 597-605.

Amoroso, G.G. and Fassina, V., 1983, "Stone decay and conservation: atmospheric pollution, cleaning, consolidation and protection", *Materials Science Monographs*, Vol 11, Elsevier, Amsterdam.

Andrew, C.A., 1992, "Towards an aesthetic theory of building soiling", in Webster, R.G.M. (Ed), Stonecleaning and the nature, soiling and decay mechanisms of stone, Proceedings of the International Conference, Edinburgh, Scotland 1992. Donhead Publishing, 63-81.

Andrew, C.A. and Crawford, E., 1992, "Conservation and planning considerations in stone cleaning" in Webster, R.G.M. (Ed), Stonecleaning and the nature, soiling and decay mechanisms of stone, Proceedings of the International Conference, Edinburgh, Scotland 1992. Donhead Publishing. 193-198.

Ashurst, J., 1972, "Conservation of stone: cleaning natural stone buildings", *The Architects Journal*, 497-504.

Ashurst, J., 1975, "Cleaning and surface treatments: Causes of decay", *The Architects Journal*, 39-49.

Ashurst, J. and Ashurst, N., 1988, Practical Building Conservation, English Heritage Technical Handbook, Vol. 1, Stone Masonry.

Black, E.L., 1977, "Cleaning sandstone buildings", *The Building Economist*, **15**, 214-217.

Bluck, B.J. and Porter, J., 1991, "Sandstone buildings and cleaning problems", *Stone Industries*, **26** (2), March 1991, 21-27.

Bravery, A.F., 1982, "Preservation in the construction industry", in Russell, A.D., Hugo, W.B. and Ayliffe, G.A.J. (Eds) Principles and Practice of Disinfection, Preservation and Sterilisation. Blackwell Scientific Publications. Oxford.

BRE, 1992, "Control of lichens, moulds and similar growths", Digest 370.

Brimblecome, P., 1992, A brief history of grime: accumulation and removal of soot deposits on buildings since the 17th century, in Webster, R.G.M. (Ed), Stonecleaning and the nature, soiling and decay mechanisms of stone. Proceedings of the International Conference, Edinburgh, Scotland 1992. Donhead Publishing. 53-62.

British Standards Institution, 1976, Code of practice for stone masonry, BS5390:1976

Cullen, G., 1961, The concise townscape. London: Architectural Press.

Danin, A. and Caneva, G., 1990, "Deterioration of limestone walls in Jerusalem and marble monuments in Rome caused by cyanbacteria and cyanophilous lichens", *International Biodeterioration*, **26**, 397-417.

Dixon, J. 1993, in Grainger, J.D. " Report of a Public Inquiry into an appeal by The City of Edinburgh District Council against the refusal of listed building consent for stone cleaning of the Scott Monument, Princes Street Gardens, Edinburgh"

Goudie, A.S., 1986, "Laboratory simulation of the "wick effect" in salt weathering of rock", *Earth Surface Processes and Landforms*, **11**, 275-285.

Grant, C., 1982, 'Fouling of terrestrial substrates by algae and implications for control - a review. *International Biodeterioration Bulletin*, **18** (3), 57-65.

Greensmith, J.T., 1979, "Petrology of the sedimentary rocks", Allen & Unwin : London.

Hicks, B.B., 1982, "Wet and dry surface deposition of pollutants and their modelling", in Conservation of Historic Stone Buildings and Monuments, National Academy Press, Washington, 183-196.

Historic Scotland, 1993, Memorandum of Guidance on Listed Buildings and Conservation Areas.

John, D.M., 1988, "Algal growths on buildings : a general review and methods of treatment", *Biodeterioration Abstracts*, **2**, (2), 81-102.

Koestler, R.J., Charola, A.E., Wypyski, M. and Lee, J.J., 1985, "Microbiologically induced deterioration of dolomitic and calcitic stone as viewed by scanning electron microscopy", in Vth International Congress on Deterioration and Conservation of Stone, Lausanne, 25-27.9.1985, 617-626.

Leary,E., 1986, "The building sandstones of the British Isles" Building Research Establishment Report.

Lewin, S.Z., 1982, "The mechanism of masonry decay through crystallisation", in Conservation of Historic Stone Buildings and Monuments, National Academy Press, Washington, 120-144.

Lynch, K., 1960, The Image of the City. Cambridge, Massachusetts: MIT Press.

MacDonald,J. and Tonge, K. 1993, "Effects of chemical cleaning processes on Scottish sandstones", in Conservation science in the U.K. , reprints of the meeting held in Glasgow, May 1993, (Ed) N.H. Tennent, James and James

Pettijohn, F.J., Potter P.E. and Siever, R., 1983, Sand and Sandstone. Berlin, Springer-Verlag.

Richardson, B.A., 1973, Control of biological growths, *Stone Industries*, **8** (2), 2-6.

Richardson, B.A., 1975, Control of moss, lichen and algae on stone, in, Rossi-Manaresi, I, (Eds) The Conservation of Stone. Proceedings of the International Symposium, Bologna, Italy.

Richardson, B.A., 1991, Defects and deterioration in buildings. Chapman and Hall, London.

Schaffer, R.J., 1932, "The weathering of building stone", BRE Special Publication No. 18, HMSO

Snethlage, R.,1985, "Hygric and thermal properties as criteria for the selection of natural stone exchange material", in Felix, G., (Ed) Proceedings of the 5th International Congress on Deterioration and Conservation of stone, Lausanne, September 1985.

Sperling, C.H.B. and Cooke, R.N., 1985, "Laboratory simulation of rock weathering by salt crystallization and hydration process in hot, arid environments", *Earh Surface Processes and Landforms*, **10**, 541-555.

Sramek , J., 1980, Determination of the source of surface deterioration on tombstones at the old Jewish cemetary in Prague, *Studies in Conservation*, **25**, 47-52.

Urquhart, D.C.M., MacDonald, J., Tongue, K., Webster, R.G.M., and Young, M.E., 1992, " Sandstone cleaning: A risk assessment", Building Pathology, International Conference on Building Pathology, Cambridge, September, 1992.

Verhoef, L.G.W., 1988, Soiling and cleaning of building facades. Chapman and Hall, London.

Webster, R.G.M. (Ed), 1992, Stonecleaning and the nature, soiling and decay mechanisms of stone, Proceedings of the International Conference, Edinburgh, Scotland. Donhead Publishing.

Webster, R., Andrew, C., Baxter, S., MacDonald, J., Rocha, M., Thomson, B., Tonge, K., Urquart, D., Young, M.E. 1992, "Stonecleaning in Scotland" Research Reports 1,2,3. Gilcomston Litho: Aberdeen.

Williams, R.B.G. and Robinson, D.A., 1981, "Weathering of sandstone by the combined action of frost and salt", *Earth Surface Processes and Landforms*, **6**, 1-9.

Young, M. and Urquhart, D. 1991, "Abrasive cleaning of sandstone buildings and monuments: an experimental investigation" in Webster, R.G.M. (Ed), Stonecleaning and the nature, soiling and decay mechanisms of stone, Proceedings of the International Conference, Edinburgh, Scotland, Donhead Publishing,128-140.